ANESTHETICS

ABDO
Publishing Company

ANESTHETICS

by Stephen Burgdorf

Content Consultant

Kumar Belani, MD
Professor, Department of Anesthesiology
University of Minnesota

✚ Credits

Published by ABDO Publishing Company, PO Box 398166, Minneapolis, MN 55439. Copyright © 2014 by Abdo Consulting Group, Inc. International copyrights reserved in all countries. No part of this book may be reproduced in any form without written permission from the publisher. The Essential Library™ is a trademark and logo of ABDO Publishing Company.

Printed in the United States of America,
North Mankato, Minnesota
062013
092013

Editor: Melissa York
Series Designer: Craig Hinton

Photo Credits: Africa Studio/Shutterstock Images, cover; Lokalin Ilya/Shutterstock Images, cover; iStockphoto/Thinkstock, cover, 14, 18, 37, 57, 61, 81, 91; Shutterstock Images, cover, 17, 51; Science & Society Picture Library/Getty Images, 7; Universal History Archive/Getty Images, 10; MENDIL/BSIP/SuperStock, 21; Custom Medical Stock Photo, 24, 27, 69; Hulton Archive/Getty Images, 28; North Wind/North Wind Picture Archives, 32; AP Images, 34; Juan Karita/AP Images, 43; Alila Medical Images/Shutterstock Images, 46; Nucleus Medical Art Inc./Alamy, 54; Abdul Khaliq/AP Images, 59; Paul W. Gillespie/AP Images, 65; Jacqueline Watson/Shutterstock Images, 71; Ray Carson/The University of Florida/AP Images, 72; Kim Brent/Monroe Evening News/AP Images, 74; Stockbyte/Thinkstock, 77; P. Holm/AP Images, 83; Dennis Sabo/Shutterstock Images, 86; John Hart/Wisconsin State Journal/AP Images, 89; Mike Derer/AP Images, 93; Dean Curtis/The Springfield News-Leader/AP Images, 97

Library of Congress Control Number: 2013932972

Cataloging-in-Publication Data

Burgdorf, Stephen.
 Anesthetics / Stephen Burgdorf.
  p. cm. -- (Medical marvels)
Includes bibliographical references and index.
ISBN 978-1-61783-900-9
1. Anesthesia--Juvenile literature. 2. Anesthetics--Juvenile literature. I. Title.
617.9--dc23

Contents

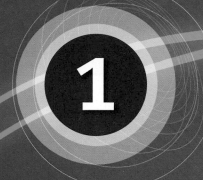

Oral Surgery:
Past and Present

The discovery of anesthetics changed the practice of medicine and the way people face pain. It also proved lucky for the ailing Eben Frost. On an early fall evening in 1846, Frost sought out Dr. William T. G. Morton in Boston, Massachusetts. He wanted help relieving one of life's occasional annoyances—tooth pain. Before the advent of reliable anesthesia, there was little to ease the pain of injuries or surgery. On September 30, Frost contacted Morton to perform a tooth extraction because his tooth pain was becoming unbearable. A desperate Frost first suggested mesmerism, or hypnotism, to block the surgical pain. But Morton had something better. He suggested using the chemical ether instead. He soaked a rag with the colorless, strong-smelling liquid and held it to Frost's face until he became unconscious. It was a crude method but successful nonetheless, as Morton removed Frost's tooth without causing the patient pain.

Dr. William Morton used ether to remove patients' teeth painlessly.

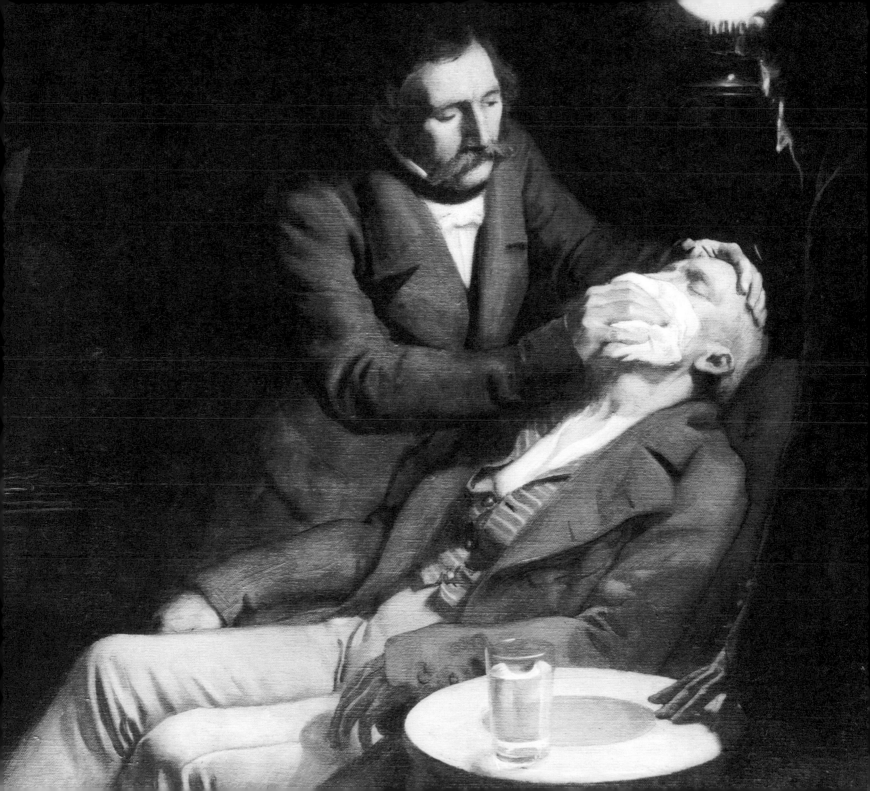

The Ether Controversy

Although Morton performed the first public demonstration of ether in surgery, there is controversy over who discovered it. Dr. Crawford Long of Georgia worked with ether in March 1842, documenting in his research that he used ether on James Venable to remove a tumor. However, he failed to publicize this to the scientific community. Dentist Horace Wells had already performed successful tooth extractions using nitrous oxide as a dental anesthetic. However, when Wells later experimented with ether before witnesses in 1845, his patient screamed out in pain as the surgery began. The audience booed him out of the surgical arena. Later, the patient admitted he hadn't felt anything.

Days after Morton's demonstration in 1846, Wells, Morton, and Morton's teacher, Dr. Charles T. Jackson, all claimed to have discovered anesthesia. Years progressed while Crawford Long's name was barely mentioned. In 1920, the New York University Hall of Fame voted Morton as the discoverer, although history reflects otherwise. Despite this controversy, the work of these giants laid the foundation for future studies of anesthetics.

Only two weeks later, Morton administered ether once again. His test case this time was Gilbert Abbott, a patient of Dr. John Warren of Massachusetts General Hospital. This was a more invasive surgery, however, since Abbott was having a tumor removed from his neck. This time Morton used a glass inhaler to administer the vapor. Before he affixed the inhaler mouthpiece to Abbott, he tried reassuring him, even bringing Frost along to the surgery. Abbott lay with his tall, thin body dangling over the edge of the operating chair. On October 16, 1846, in front of onlooking surgeons, Morton performed the first public demonstration of ether. Warren performed successful surgery on the nonresisting patient, impressing the critical but professional audience.

Before ether was discovered, doctors seldom used pain relievers during surgery. They operated only when not performing surgery would mean certain death. Risk was high, and patients hoped for a quick procedure. If surgery took too long they could exhaust themselves writhing in pain and go into shock. Some chose suicide rather than seemingly torturous surgery with no pain relief. Others chose to live with a condition that killed them slowly. The anesthetic options were limited to alcohol, the drug opium, tourniquets (cloth or rubber bands tied tightly to cut off blood circulation), or ice. A team of surgical assistants held down the patient during surgery.

Drinking alcohol usually resulted in sickness and vomiting before achieving blood levels that would dull the pain of surgery. Opium, a drug made from poppy seeds, was also too slow to take effect. It provided analgesia (pain relief) but not anesthesia (loss of sensation). Opium use also caused significant side effects including dangerously slow breathing, and it could be physically addicting. Written in 1812, *A Treatise*

Hypnotism

In the early 1800s, mesmerism, or hypnotism, gained popularity in Great Britain as a way to perform painless surgery. Hypnotism causes a trancelike state that leaves patients relaxed and calm. Patients endured surgical procedures such as mastectomies, tooth pullings, amputations, and even childbirth "without pain in the mesmeric state."[1] By the late 1800s, the practice of mesmerism decreased as use of anesthetics became standard.

Serratura.

of the Operations of Surgery suggests patients "bite down on a piece of wood" while having their leg amputated. It also suggests surgeries be performed in the spring or fall, as the warmer temperatures revive the blood better in the spring and in the fall the blood is "calmer."[2] Some doctors took barbaric measures, giving patients a hard blow to the face to knock them out. Unfortunately, these methods were imprecise and seldom helped the patients endure surgery. Usually the patient still experienced agonizing pain.

Ether, although effective, had serious risks. It was extremely combustible. The available techniques did not allow doctors to control the ether dose. It also required the patient continue breathing on his own. He needed to continue taking in the fumes so he did not wake up during surgery. On the other hand, an overdose could cause loss of brain activity, heart failure, and death.

Dental Surgery Today

Today, dental patients have several options. They do not have to worry about inhaling chemicals on a rag before they undertake a procedure. They rest in comfortable dental chairs while practitioners calm their anxiety. Patients expect a comfortable and painless procedure with a quick recovery.

A surgeon's assistant with a padded hand stands ready to punch out the patient during a leg amputation in this 1600s woodcut.

If Frost had his tooth pulled today, he would have received an injection of a local anesthetic near his extraction area. He would have witnessed the whole procedure, too. Instead, Frost received a form of general anesthesia, rendering him unconscious.

Imagine if Frost traveled through time to 2014. An oral surgeon first tucks a cotton swab inside his cheek. The cotton holds a dab of the gel anesthetic benzocaine. This lessens the sting of the needle before he receives the primary anesthetic through a syringe. A sting, or any other form of pain, results when certain chemicals try to enter nerve endings. An anesthetic is like a dam, preventing this process from occurring and blocking the pain. Within minutes, he feels a tingly numbness in the swabbed area.

Next, Frost will receive a common dental anesthetic such as lidocaine. Thanks to the benzocaine gel, he will feel only a tugging sensation and a slight sting when the needle is carefully inserted into his jaw near the surgical area. The surgeon carefully dispenses drops of the anesthetic with gentle, quick precision. Before Frost can become uneasy, the surgeon is done and has placed the needle back on the tray. Lidocaine quickly blocks stronger pain—the surgeon's pliers, drill, and metal pick. Immediately, the chemicals in the anesthetic react with the nerves in the localized area. They block even more nerve endings and cause the loss of multiple sensations. First, Frost will lose all feeling of pain, including sensations of hot or cold. Next, he will lose the sense of deep pressure in the medicated area, and finally, he will be unable to move his mouth. Despite the funny feeling in his face, he will be awake and alert.

Surgery is about to start. Frost is ready after receiving a quick, comfortable anesthesia procedure with fast-acting anesthetics and a reassuring dental staff. The surgeon chooses his first instruments and after a few cracks, tugs, and scrapes, he removes the tooth. The short procedure is over much more quickly than the methodical pain-dulling process. In fact, pulling Frost's lone tooth took only minutes. The anesthetic will last long after the surgery is over. Benzocaine wears off quickly. However, lidocaine lasts up to five hours, depending on the concentration and dose.[3] Eventually Frost regains feeling in his mouth, but he will still have some post-surgery aches in his jaw. He will be given a prescription for an analgesic pain reliever, which is an anesthetic designed for blocking pain.

Dental anesthetics and their delivery methods have evolved greatly over the past 150 years—from crude and experimental to precise and practiced. The reason, however,

The Last Resort

Statistics illustrate how surgery truly was a last resort before anesthesia. From 1821 to 1846, the Massachusetts General Hospital recorded only 333 surgeries, which amounted to fewer than one per month. In 1897, an elderly Boston physician shared horrible memories of "yells and screams" during surgeries from the years before anesthesia and the desperate measures taken to induce any type of pain dulling or unconsciousness.[4]

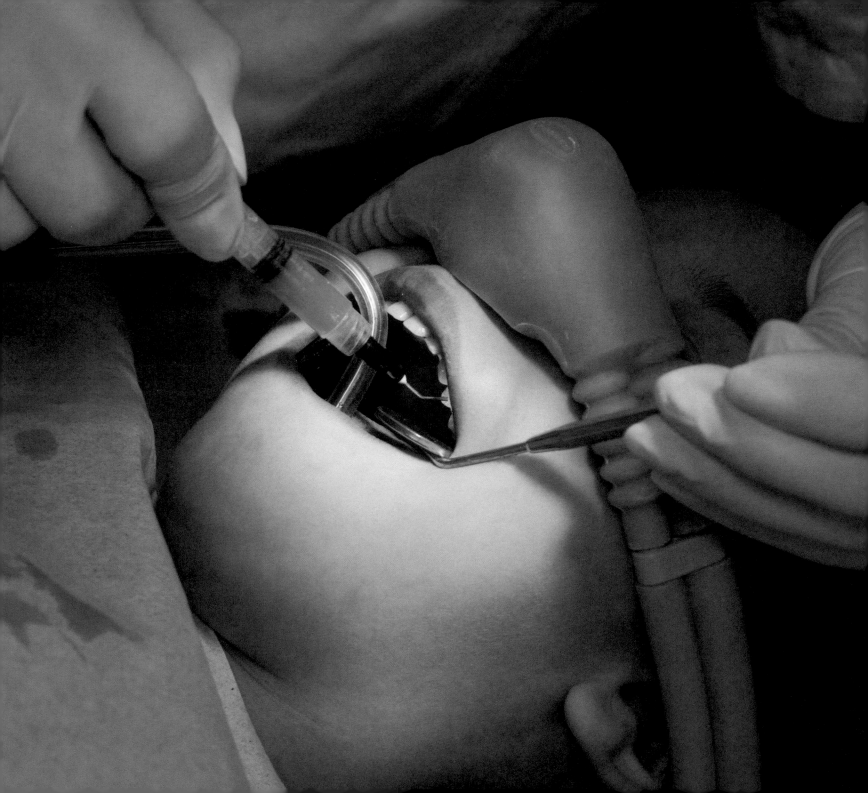

General anesthetics render the entire body unconscious. Local anesthetics block sensations in localized, or specific, areas of the body, primarily pain, but also feeling and sometimes movement.

has always been the same: to prevent pain. Oral surgery is just one example in a long and growing list of surgical procedures. Whatever the type of surgery, all require some form of anesthetic to block sensations and allow surgeons to perform safe, life-saving procedures.

 Dental surgeons today can choose local or general anesthesia or both to make their patients comfortable during procedures.

How Anesthetics Work

Oral surgery is just one of many the procedures performed every day that requires some form of anesthetic to help block sensations, usually pain. The word *anesthesia* originates from the Greek words *an* (without) and *aesthesis* (sensation). In simplest terms, anesthetics stop the transmission of signals to the brain, which the brain interprets as sensations. During anesthesia, patients can experience many sensations, including unconsciousness, immobility, analgesia, or amnesia, depending on the type of anesthetic.

Anesthetics interfere with the working of the body's nervous system, which controls conscious and unconscious body processes. Under the skin, embedded in the body tissues and organs, are millions of nerve endings. After a drug is inhaled, injected, or rubbed on, it begins seeping into

Unconsciousness is one of several possible effects of anesthesia.

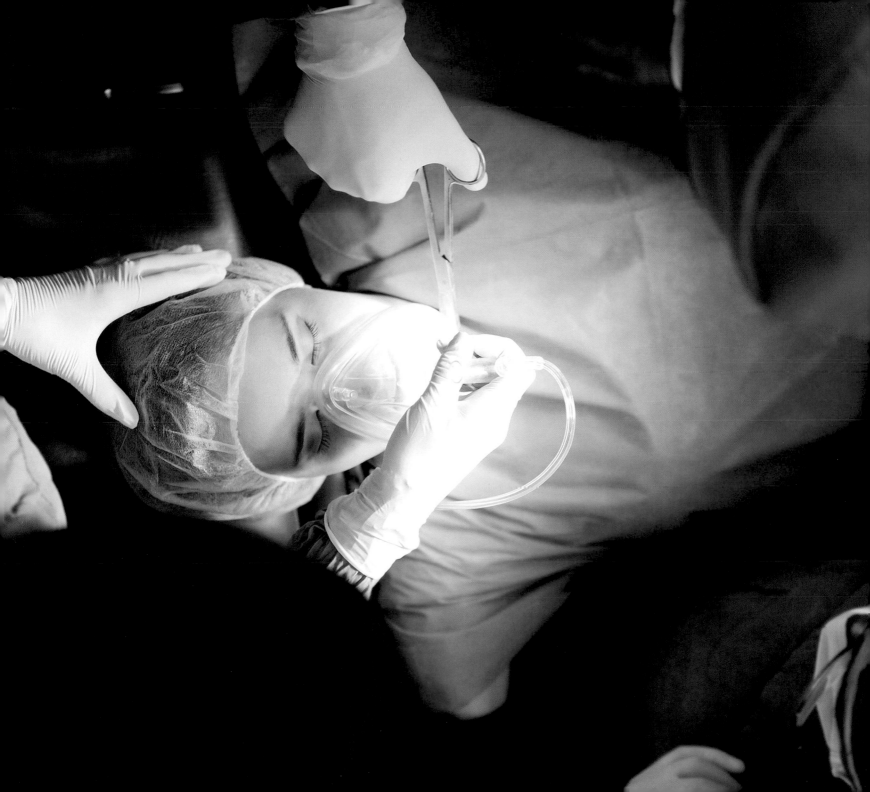

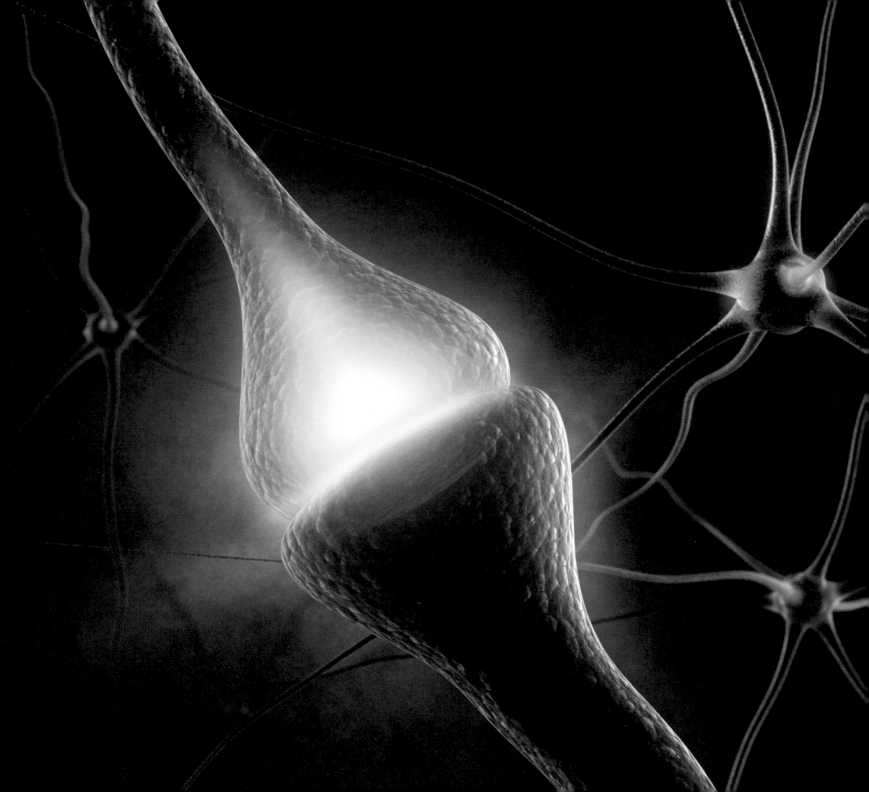

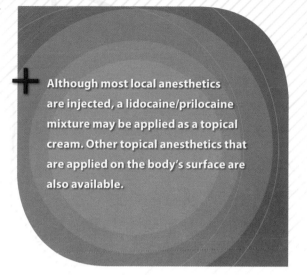

Although most local anesthetics are injected, a lidocaine/prilocaine mixture may be applied as a topical cream. Other topical anesthetics that are applied on the body's surface are also available.

the nerve endings through the fatty skin and organ tissues and the bloodstream. Soon the body reacts. These processes are the pharmacology traits of anesthetics, broken into two principles: pharmacokinetics (how the body's systems process drugs) and pharmacodynamics (how drugs affect the body's systems).

How the Body Processes Drugs

Surgery patients receive anesthetics by many different routes, but the main purpose is the same: to work as effectively and efficiently as possible. General anesthetic gases, such as isoflurane, are breathed in through an inhaler mask. The mask allows the anesthesiologist to regulate the release of the gas. Local anesthetics such as lidocaine come typically by means of an intravenous (IV) injection. Some anesthetics are swallowed as pills or a liquid.

Chemicals or electric impulses transmit between nerve cells at their synapses, *in green*. Some anesthetics work by slowing these transmissions.

Administration and Absorption

There are four ways anesthetics are administered.

+ Enterally: the anesthetic is swallowed or otherwise passed through the digestive system.

+ Parenterally: the anesthetic is injected and does not pass through the digestive system.

+ Inhalation: the anesthetic passes through the mouth but is absorbed by the respiratory system and not the digestive system.

+ Topically: the anesthetic is applied on the body.

Each of these methods has advantages and disadvantages. A disadvantage of enteral drugs is their first pass effect. The first pass effect describes how much medicine is lost when drugs pass through the liver before reaching the bloodstream and the rest of the body. IV drugs, since they are administered directly to the bloodstream, act more quickly and have little or no first pass effect. Regardless of the type and administration method of the anesthetic, the drug begins to work once it is absorbed.

Distribution

Once an anesthetic is absorbed into the bloodstream, it travels through numerous tiny capillaries to the rest of the body. The blood carrying the anesthetic reaches three types of tissue—organs, muscle,

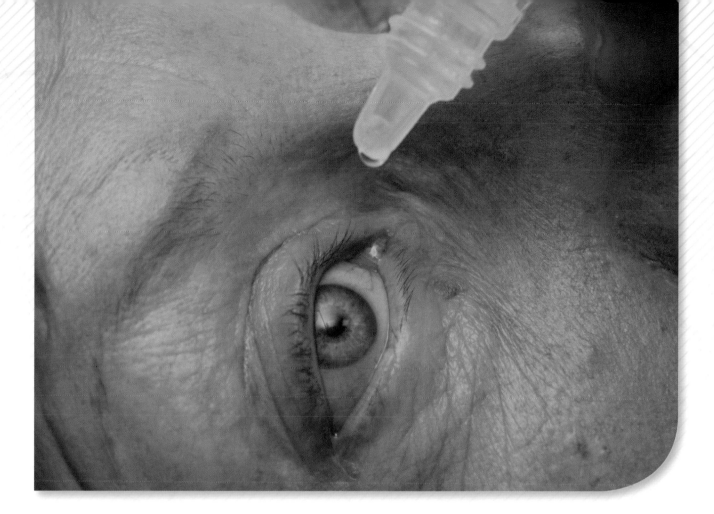

and fat. Blood flows in different volumes to each type. The brain, heart, kidneys, and liver have a high number of blood vessels, which make blood flow greater in these areas. This causes the traveling drug to reach these organs first. Therefore, these organs receive the highest percentage of a dose. Later, the

Urine Drug Tests

Drug residues exist in the highest concentrations in urine. Many drugs can be detected in urine for a relatively long period of time after they are administered. The drugs also linger even if the sample has been in storage. A person's kidney and liver functions can affect urine drug levels, as can the type of drug. Drugs such as codeine, morphine, and cocaine are detectable for only one to three days. In contrast, marijuana is detectable for up to 60 days after its use.[1]

drug distributes to bulky muscle and fat groups and those with fewer blood vessels. Last, the drug is broken down by the liver to leave the body as waste or else is eliminated unchanged.

How the Drug Affects the Body

The body processes anesthetics on a microscopic, molecular level. These processes are invisible, unseen by humans, occurring as the drug is absorbed, distributed, and eliminated from the body. Once the drug is in the body, it begins to interact with specific nerve receptors, initiating the body's natural chemical reactions. This process is known as agonism. In agonism, the drug binds to receptors to produce maximum response. In partial agonism, the drug binds to receptors to produce lesser response. And in antagonism, the drug binds to the receptors but blocks responses.

Anesthesia is not without risk, even with trained anesthesiologists administering drugs using modern techniques and equipment. This is because each patient is unique and will respond differently based on health status and the type of surgery. That is why complications can occur. Most of the time, side effects of general anesthesia are tolerable and mild, including nausea and vomiting after general anesthesia, sore throat, and pain because of surgery. Less likely but severe risks include brain damage, nerve injury, and even death.

Regional and local anesthesia carry their own sets of risks, too. A regional anesthetic is similar to a local anesthetic, but it affects a larger region of the body. Local anesthesia patients can experience infection or nerve injury and bleeding from needles. Spinal anesthesia, a regional anesthetic technique, can sometimes cause respiratory failure, usually due to overdose.

The Study of Pain

According to the International Association for the Study of Pain (IASP), pain is defined as "an unpleasant sensory and emotional experience associated with actual or potential tissue damage."[2] Researchers in anesthesiology are often involved in the study of pain. Pain may be experienced in different parts of the body as sharp, burning, pinprick, itching, dull, or aching. There is somatic pain, which occurs in the skin, muscles, and joints. There is visceral pain, which happens in the internal organs. Neuropathic pain is a tingly sensation followed by a burning sensation, or what it feels like when you bash your elbow. By learning how pain works within the nervous system and where it is located, anesthesiologists can determine the best types of anesthetics and the most effective methods.

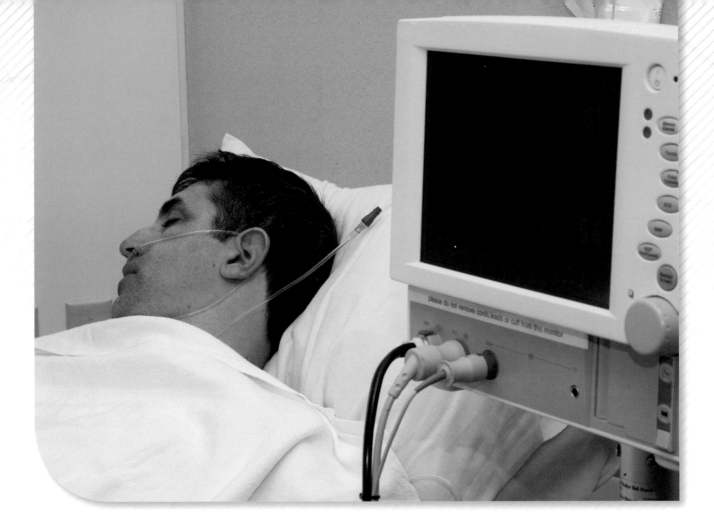

Sometimes, a complication may occur after a procedure is completed and the anesthetic has worn off. The drugs' chemical reactions do not always work as planned. Organ toxicity happens when the vital organs have been exposed to certain toxins that result from the breakdown of the anesthetic. This

Patients require recovery time to wake up from general anesthesia.

People with red hair feel pain more strongly than people with any other hair color. The same genes that control red hair color also control sensitivity to pain. It can take 20 percent more anesthesia to put redheads under than brunettes.[3]

condition, although rare, is commonly associated with certain inhaled general anesthetics. It usually results in liver toxicity and liver failure, both of which can be fatal. Age, obesity, and long exposure to the anesthetic contribute to liver toxicity.

General Anesthesia: Going to Sleep

Commonly known as "going to sleep" or "going under," general anesthesia is defined as the generalized depression, or slowing down, of the central nervous system. It results in amnesia, analgesia, unconsciousness, and immobility. Today's patients achieve general anesthesia when one or both types of general anesthetics, inhaled and IV, are administered.

Dr. Morton's famous tooth extraction displayed the effects of the volatile liquid ether. Ether emits vapors that have powerful anesthetic effects. This gas is so strong it left Morton's patients comatose, depressing their central nervous system. They became unconscious, immobile, and pain-free. As ether was used more and more in the United States, another volatile gas, chloroform, was gaining popularity in Great Britain.

Some general anesthetics are given intravenously.

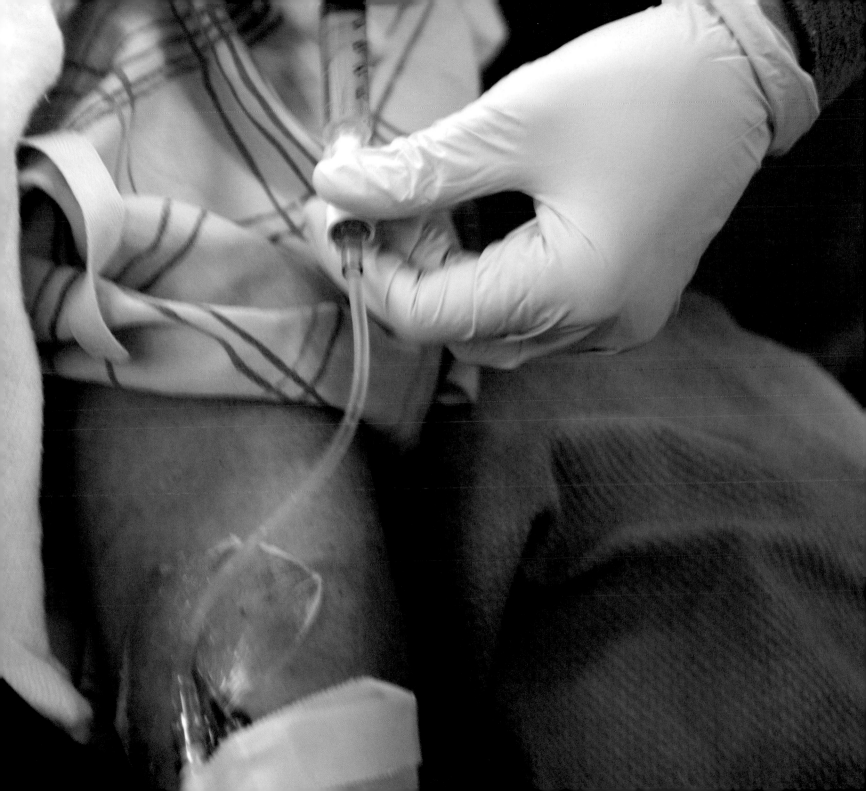

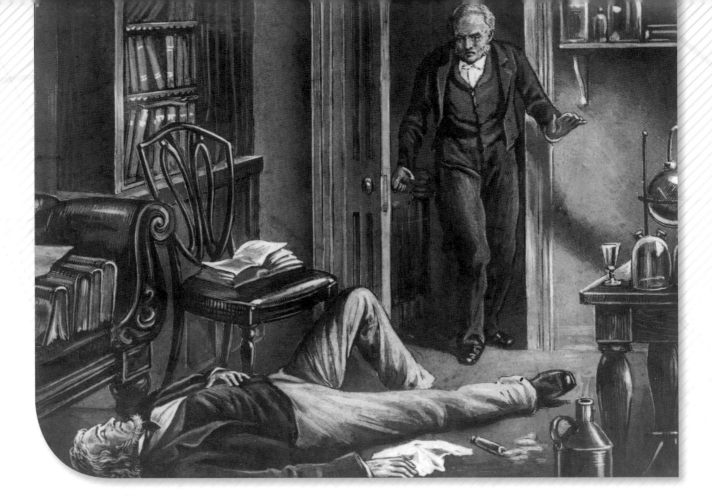

Chloroform

Chloroform was once considered a good replacement for ether, which was unpleasant to inhale, combustible, and explosive. Scottish obstetrician James Simpson sought a replacement for ether. He

inhaled chloroform and discovered it had similar effects. As an obstetrician, he was aware of the pain women experienced during childbirth. Simpson believed it was immoral for women to have to endure the pain. He argued for the use of anesthesia in labor and delivery, and in 1847, he delivered the first baby with the mother under chloroform. The public began to take notice, including author Charles Dickens and scientist Charles Darwin. News of chloroform reached Queen Victoria in England, and she used it for the delivery of her last two children.

However, when a 15-year-old girl died while having her toenail extracted while under chloroform in 1848, the medical profession began a deeper study of the colorless liquid. As the 1800s wore on, stories of the dangers of chloroform became widely known. The death toll mounted from patients inhaling the substance. Doctors found it could cause permanent liver damage, as well as heart failure and death. Graphic crime stories associated it with abductions, rapes, and other criminal activities. This public fear of chloroform resulted in increased fear of all anesthesia as the deaths and criminal associations set into public consciousness. In the late 1800s, British surgeon Frederick Treves believed "the majority of patients regarded the anaesthetic with far greater dread than the operation."[1]

In the late 1800s and early 1900s, committees began investigating the effects of chloroform. Studies continued to advocate for its use, but as this happened, deaths increased. In 1912, the American

Bite the Bullet

Today, the phrase "bite the bullet" is used when a person does something even though he or she does not want to. Some believe this phrase originates from soldiers actually biting on bullets to help them endure battlefield surgery during the American Civil War (1861– 1865). This is despite the fact that chloroform was used to provide relief on both sides of the battle. Approximately 80,000 Union and Confederate soldiers received chloroform.[3] It was hard for Confederate soldiers to acquire supplies of chloroform at times. In 1862, during the battle of Winchester, General Thomas Jonathan "Stonewall" Jackson captured 15,000 cases of the anesthetic for the South.[4]

Medical Association Committee on Anesthesia deemed chloroform "too risky."[2] Today, chloroform is no longer used as an anesthetic.

Anesthetic Gases

Today, one common method of administering anesthetics is through inhalation, or having the patient breathe a gas. Inhalation anesthetics are divided into two types: nitrous oxide and halogenated agents.

Nitrous oxide, more commonly called laughing gas, makes patients less anxious and less aware of pain. Halogenated agents, including halothane, sevoflurane, isoflurane, enflurane, and desflurane, were developed in the 1900s. Halogenated agents are less flammable and less toxic vapors than ether or chloroform.

Nitrous Oxide

Nitrous oxide was discovered by accident. It happened sometime between 1771 and 1777. The exact date is not known because its discoverer, Sir Joseph Priestley, was not exactly sure what he had. Priestley's gas was created from a mix of iron filings, sulfur, and water. The British scientist called it "dephlogisticated nitrous air."[5] Close to the end of the century, another experimenter, Humphrey Davy, inhaled nitrous oxide and enjoyed many experiments with it, recording "overwhelming joy" and "most voluptuous [sensuous] sensations."[6] Davy experimented further and even relieved a toothache by inhaling the gas, but he did not realize the significance of his discovery. He never published his findings.

In 1844, Gardner Colton hosted an exhibition in Connecticut to demonstrate the effects of nitrous oxide. His presentation caught the eye of the dentist Horace Wells. Wells was intrigued by the lack of responsiveness in Colton's

Nitrous Oxide Relaxation

In addition to its pain-blocking properties, nitrous oxide is popular in dental offices as an antianxiety drug. Taking nitrous oxide helps patients, especially children, feel better overall. Patients may drop their shoulders or uncross their legs as a sign of their induced relaxation. Their eye movements will slow, perhaps losing focus on the surgeon, and their eyes might appear glazed or glossy. Smiling comes easily as the face loses tension.

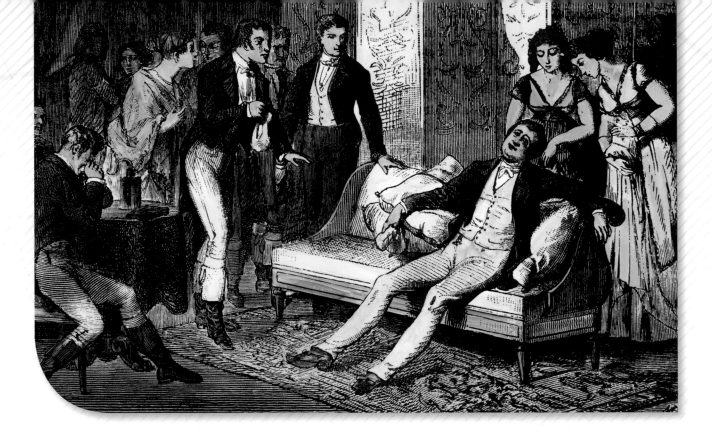

patients. He wondered if the gas could be used as a dental analgesic. He wanted to try it on himself. The next day, Wells inhaled nitrous oxide and a colleague pulled one of his teeth. It was a success, and Wells began using nitrous oxide in dental procedures. Dentists took notice of nitrous oxide, and it became a standard for pain relief.

Nitrous oxide remains popular today because it relieves pain and helps manage anxiety. Additionally, nitrous oxide has amnestic properties. Patients do not recall the severity of pain, and they

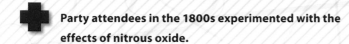
experience an altered sense of time. Nitrous oxide is the weakest of the inhaled agents. It can also be combined with other inhalants. This reduces the amount of other gases used and lessens the risk of toxic effects.

Halogenated Gases: Halothane and Sevoflurane

In 1956, halothane was introduced as a new, safer anesthetic agent. It did not have the flammability of ether, and it was less toxic than chloroform. As a result of halothane's success, competing pharmaceutical companies raced to develop even more potent but safer anesthetic gases. Scientists worked to decrease adverse effects such as circulatory or respiratory problems and improve recovery time from anesthesia. Halothane is not as commonly used today in the United States because of its risk of liver toxicity. However, many developing countries still use it because of its low price.

+ Ether Parties

In the early 1800s, there were no radios or movies for entertainment. People held social gatherings such as square dances, quilt parties, and candy pullings. Supplementing these gatherings were ether parties, where people gathered to sniff ether or nitrous oxide to get high. Showmen would travel the country with the gas, demonstrating to crowds the effects of nitrous oxide.

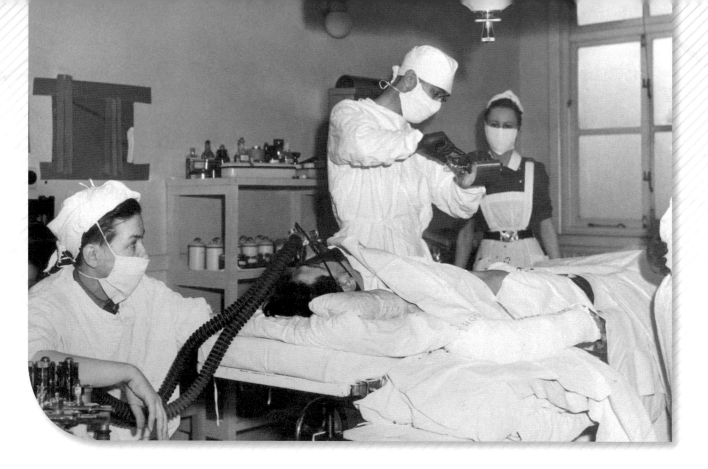

Sevoflurane was developed from and shares many of the same chemical properties as halothane. It is a relatively safe gas compared to other anesthetic gases, such as isoflurane, enflurane, and desflurane. Unlike these gases, sevoflurane does not irritate the throat. This minimizes coughing, breath holding, excess saliva, and throat spasms. It is also pleasant smelling. According to studies, overall it is a smoother gas to inhale than other halogenated gases. Compared to halothane, it is quicker to wake up from once

the anesthetic begins to wear off. This makes it popular for children's procedures. Sevoflurane acts quickly, with patients losing consciousness in less than two minutes.[7] However, because of its rapid recovery, patients can awaken agitated or delirious.

Intravenous General Anesthetics

IV anesthetics are injected directly in to the bloodstream. This has become the most common way of inducting general anesthesia. Some of these anesthetics are administered using an IV drip while others are injected via needle. IV anesthetics act on the brain and spinal cord, reaching these areas quickly through the bloodstream. Moreover, they are highly lipid soluble. This means they act quickly because they penetrate easily into the fatty cell membranes of the brain and spinal cord.

Gas Potency

The potency of anesthetic gases is measured by what is called minimum alveolar concentration (MAC). MAC compares strengths of vapors. It is defined as the amount of anesthetic gas that will prevent movement in 50 percent of subjects. Simply put, it is a way to measure an effective dose. The lower the MAC value, the more potent the gas is. Nitrous oxide carries a MAC value of 105, while the very potent isoflurane has a MAC of 1.2.[8] Factors such as age, species, and additional drugs can alter an anesthetic's MAC value.

Anesthesia and the Perception of Time

A study in the December 2012 journal *PNAS* shows how general anesthesia can affect the circadian clock of honeybees. The circadian clock regulates our daily behavior as well as our perception of time. The circadian clock of bees mimics that of mammals, so what scientists learn about bees may have an application for humans. The study concluded that general anesthesia given during the day shifts the patient's clock, inducing jet lag–like symptoms and altering time perception. Scientists hope to use this research to find better ways to help patients recover from anesthesia. This would allow them to modify anesthesia techniques to treat general anesthesia–induced jet lag.

The ideal IV anesthetic would be one that, like inhaled anesthetics, causes unconsciousness, amnesia, and analgesia. It would act quickly and be processed by the body at a rapid pace. It would be nontoxic with a minimal effect on breathing and heart rate. It would minimize organ stress while not causing brain or heart damage. It would be hypoallergenic and not cause the release of histamines, which are chemicals the body releases during an allergic response. Currently there is no single IV agent that achieves all of these effects at once.

Intravenous anesthetics were first created in the early 1900s, after the advent of hollow needles, syringes, and IV therapy (infusing substances directly into veins). Taking advantage of the new IV systems, researchers began developing new intravenous agents. Today, the most widely used IV anesthetics include barbiturates, propofol,

The development of modern syringes and needles in the 1800s made IV anesthetics possible.

etomidate, ketamine, and dexmedetomidine. Each substance has its own characteristics that make it an effective choice for anesthesia.

Barbiturates

German scientist Adolf von Baeyer synthesized the first barbiturates in the late 1800s. The first intravenous barbiturates were introduced in the early 1900s. Barbiturates have a calming effect and produce sleep by depressing the central nervous system. One of the notable pioneers in intravenous anesthetics was John Lundy of the Mayo Clinic in Minnesota, who first introduced sodium amobarbital and pentobarbital in anesthesia. Hexobarbital and thiopental were introduced in the 1930s, with hexobarbital first used for oral surgery in the United States in 1932.

Barbiturates including thiopental, thiamylal, and methohexital are used primarily for sedation and relaxation in anesthesia, as they drastically slow breathing. They were the most popular IV anesthetic choices until the 1990s, when propofol use spread. There are many types of barbiturates, and they take shorter or longer amounts of time to take effect and wear off. Categories include ultra-short, short, intermediate, and long-acting. When using barbiturates with shorter action, anesthesiologists can periodically re-dose the patient to maintain the anesthetic state. Barbiturates have weak analgesic effects. In fact, some evidence shows they could actually make patients feel pain more acutely, an effect known as antanalgesia or hyperalgesia.

Propofol

Propofol is the most commonly used IV general anesthetic today, replacing thiopental as the agent of choice for sedation. It is a thick, milky-white liquid. It induces anesthesia quickly and patients recover fast with minimal side effects after a dose wears off. Propofol drastically lowers blood pressure and suppresses breathing, requiring the patient to be continuously monitored.

Etomidate, Ketamine, and Dexmedetomidine

Etomidate is known for having less effect on the functions of the heart and lungs. However, it is not very effective in preventing convulsions. This anesthetic also carries a high risk of nausea and vomiting.

Propofol Abuse

Propofol's quick onset and lack of side effects has made it a popular choice for patients undergoing surgery. However, it is seeing increasing abuse among health-care professionals using the drug improperly as a sleep aid. In June 2009, pop star Michael Jackson died from a large dose of propofol.

IV Anesthetics Quick Facts

Anesthetic	Date of Discovery	Benefits	Drawbacks
barbiturates	Late 1800s	Brain protection; prevents seizures; inexpensive	Painful to inject; nausea and vomiting; weak analgesic
propofol	Introduced for clinical use in 1977	Does not cause nausea/vomiting; quick induction and recovery	Painful to inject; expensive; lowers heart rate the most of common general anesthetics
etomidate	Introduced in 1972	Limited effect on lung and heart function	Does not prevent seizures; nausea and vomiting; painful to inject
ketamine	Developed in 1962; used clinically since 1970	Does not require an IV; does not interfere with lung or heart function	Nausea and vomiting; can cause hallucinations when the patient is waking up
dexmedetomidine	Introduced in 1999	Does not interfere with lung function; low organ toxicity	Can cause low blood pressure and slow heart rate

Ketamine is used as an anesthetic for humans and animals. It sedates patients while preserving heart activity and respiration. Other anesthetics often hinder these functions. These unique characteristics have made ketamine a good anesthetic choice for children and patients with heart conditions or asthma. Ketamine can be given intravenously, intramuscularly (in a muscle), orally (in the mouth), rectally (in the rectum), or nasally (in the nose). It is in a class of anesthetic drugs known as dissociative anesthetics. These drugs distort the user's perception of sight and sound and produce feelings of detachment from one's environment and self.

Dexmedetomidine is a newer sedative analgesic. It only minimally slows breathing when administered in appropriate doses. It has very little organ toxicity. Similar to ketamine, it promotes pain relief while inducing sedation. However, it does slow patients' heart rates.

 PCP

Ketamine's effects are similar to those of an illegal drug known as phencyclidine (PCP). Like ketamine, PCP itself was once used as an anesthetic. However, it was discontinued because its effects were frequent and severe. Ketamine is chemically similar to PCP, and it is still used illegally without a prescription. Its street name is Special K.

Local Anesthetics:
Alert, Without Sensation

As scientists developed general anesthetic drugs in the mid-1800s, a new type of anesthetic, cocaine, was also being developed from the leaves of the coca plant. This plant grows in the Andes Mountains of Peru and Bolivia. The indigenous people chew its leaves as a stimulant, as an appetite suppressant, and to help relieve minor aches. Throughout the rest of the century, cocaine became popular in England and the United States as a local anesthetic.

But cocaine had drawbacks. It was toxic to patients, resulting in many deaths. Also, medical staff members were becoming addicted to the drug. In the late 1800s and early 1900s, scientists began synthesizing pure cocaine. Unlike cocaine from natural sources, these new formulations were not addictive or toxic when applied near the nerves. The first injectable local anesthetic was procaine.

Chewing coca leaves is an Andean tradition.

+ Adrenaline in Anesthesia

In sports, athletes sometimes refer to the "adrenaline kicking in" during a critical performance, when hormones are released and an athlete may temporarily gain extra strength, enhanced awareness, a boost of energy, and temporary loss of pain. This is the body's natural response to high stress situations. Adrenaline, or epinephrine, is sometimes added to local anesthetics to constrict blood vessels and reduce blood loss in the localized area. Heinrich Braun, who first experimented with adrenaline in anesthetics in the early 1900s, dubbed it a "chemical tourniquet" for adrenaline's ability to constrict blood flow.[1]

Scientists were able to synthesize the newer drugs from procaine's molecular patterns, and it became the template on which all modern injectable local anesthetics are based.

What They Do

Local anesthetics act as a barrier to pain within nerve endings. They are lipid-soluble drugs, meaning they move through fat easiest. They penetrate the tissues and set up a sort of roadblock between the source of the pain, such as a scalpel incision or dentist's drill, and the brain. Once the impulse travels from the source, it never reaches the brain, denying the central nervous system the chance to process it. The result of this chemical reaction is the loss of pain in the area where the drug was injected or topically applied.

The lipid solubility of a local anesthetic determines its strength. For example, the anesthetic effects of a highly lipid-soluble local anesthetic such as ropivacaine or etidocaine lasts longer than a local anesthetic such as lidocaine or procaine with a lower lipid solubility. This does not, however, take away from their effectiveness. Surgeons adjust their dosage depending on what kind of drug they are administering.

There are factors that can affect the spread of a local anesthetic. One is nerve diameter: a smaller diameter allows the anesthetic to work more quickly. The presence of myelin, which is an insulating layer of fatty proteins that forms around a nerve, allows nerve impulses to travel faster. In turn, the local anesthetic acts quicker. When a local anesthetic is injected close to a nerve, it reaches the outer surface of the bundle of nerves first. This close proximity to the injection point results in the localized area near the injection losing sensation first. As the drug moves through the nerve tissue, it reaches the core of the bundle of nerve fibers. The nerve fibers spread out to the further reaches of the body, and thus, the drug reaches them later after it has been administered.

Regional Anesthesia

Local anesthetics are also used for regional anesthesia. This is the process of rendering a portion of the body without sensation, rather than general anesthesia, which is total unconsciousness. Regional anesthesia covers a region of the body as opposed to a smaller localized area.

Anatomy of a Nerve

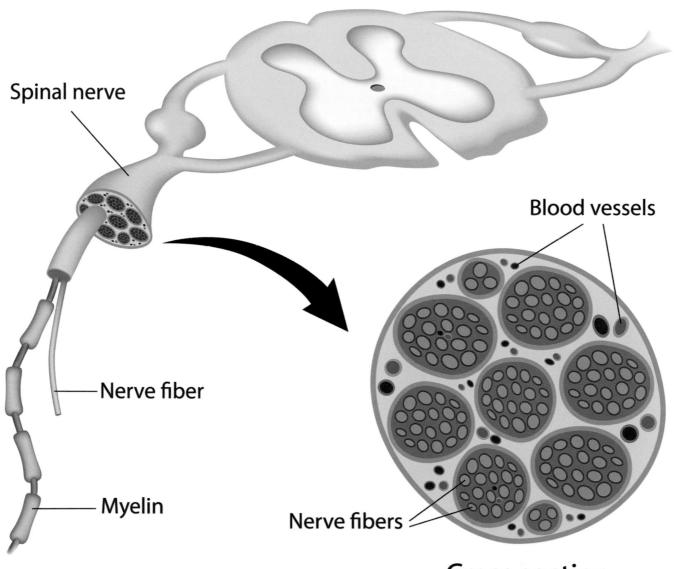

Spinal nerve

Nerve fiber

Myelin

Blood vessels

Nerve fibers

Cross section

Regional anesthetics are often used in dentistry and obstetrics. There are many specialized techniques used depending on which area of the body needs to be anesthetized. Some include peripheral nerve blocks and spinal analgesia. A peripheral nerve block affects the nerves in a local region of the body, usually the arms or legs and sometimes the neck. It is in contrast to a central nerve block, which affects all the nerves, as used in general anesthesia. During spinal analgesia, a small needle is inserted inside the spine, causing regional anesthesia starting at the rib cage and proceeding down to the toes.

Types of Local Anesthetics

There are two classifications of local anesthetic drugs: amino esters and amino amides. The difference between the two types is mostly in their chemical structure, though they are also distinguished by a few key factors. One of the most significant is their stability and storage. Esters break down more easily than amides, making them less stable and not able to be stored at length.

Amino Esters

Procaine was first used primarily as a spinal anesthetic. Today, procaine is still used in dental procedures. It can also be used in nerve block techniques. Procaine is also used as a topical analgesic. It is commonly

 The nerves that run throughout the body are bundled together. Nerves on the outside of the bundles are affected by anesthesia first.

Over-the-Counter Creams

Scan the pain relief section at the drugstore, and you will see a wide variety of gels, creams, and patches designed to "rub out" the pain. However, some say these topical drugs are not truly effective but rather operate because of the placebo effect. This means the patient's mental expectations rather than the traits of the drug are producing the results.

The drugs are absorbed into the skin and come in many varieties. Menthol gels are designed to provide a cooling sensation. Capsaicin-based gels and creams cause a burning sensation that helps relieve pain. Some familiar brands include Bengay, IcyHot, and Aspercreme.

known by its trade name, Novocain. It takes effect in less than five minutes and wears off in approximately one hour.[2]

Tetracaine, also known as amethocaine, is a potent topical gel used for local anesthesia of the skin. As an injected anesthetic, it is most popular for spinal anesthesia. It is also used infrequently for peripheral nerve blocks. Tetracaine has a slow onset time and metabolizes slowly; it typically takes five to ten minutes to take effect and lasts up to two hours.[3]

Chloroprocaine is an IV local anesthetic commonly used in childbirth and for spinal anesthesia. Unlike other local anesthetics, chloroprocaine constricts blood vessels, meaning it also decreases blood loss during surgery. It is also referred to by its trade name, Nesacaine.

Benzocaine is a low-potency local anesthetic that is commonly used to relieve pain and itching from sunburn,

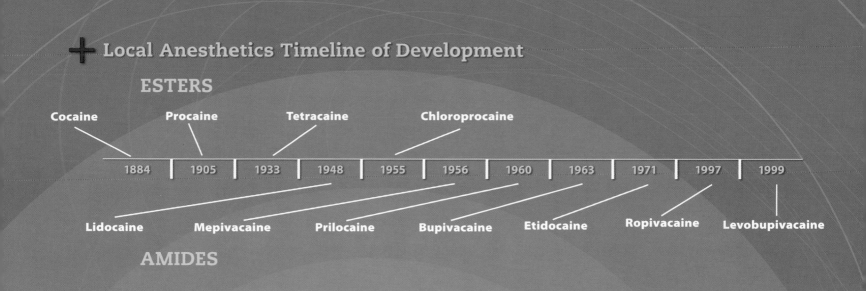

Local Anesthetics Timeline of Development

ESTERS

Cocaine — 1884
Procaine — 1905
Tetracaine — 1933
Chloroprocaine

| 1884 | 1905 | 1933 | 1948 | 1955 | 1956 | 1960 | 1963 | 1971 | 1997 | 1999 |

Lidocaine
Mepivacaine
Prilocaine
Bupivacaine
Etidocaine
Ropivacaine
Levobupivacaine

AMIDES

bug bites, poison ivy, or minor cuts and scratches. It is also the main ingredient in topical gels for teething and lozenges for sore throats.

Amino Amides

Lidocaine is the most commonly used and versatile amino-amide anesthetic. It can be administered through an IV or as a topical cream or patch. It is used frequently in dental clinics, where it has almost completely replaced procaine for tooth extractions, cavity fillings, and root canals. Since the 1950s, researchers have focused more on developing amino-amide local anesthetics because they are more shelf stable and cause fewer allergic reactions than esters.

Anesthesia Guidelines

The American Dental Society of Anesthesiology (ADA) was founded in 1954 to encourage the study of anesthesiology and promote education of anesthesia in dental schools. Over the next three decades, more groups formed to advocate for the awareness of dental anesthesia as a specialty and to establish guidelines for the delivery of sedation and anesthesia. In 1985, the first guidelines were issued, and by 1997, all states had laws in place controlling the use of general anesthesia and sedation, with 29 states regulating nitrous oxide.[6]

Local Anesthetics and Dentistry

Local anesthesia is critical for modern dentistry. Anesthesia for dental procedures is known as office-based anesthesia, meaning patients are sent home on the day of treatment, and procedures are done outside the hospital. Most dental work is minimally invasive, with the exception of extensive oral surgery procedures such as multiple wisdom tooth extractions. Oral surgery accounts for the most anesthetics or sedations administered, averaging 5 million per year.[4]

Phobia of dentistry pain is rooted in society, engrained in the minds of people at an early age. Even today, with advanced techniques, technology, and anesthetic agents, dentistry remains an anxiety-provoking procedure. Half

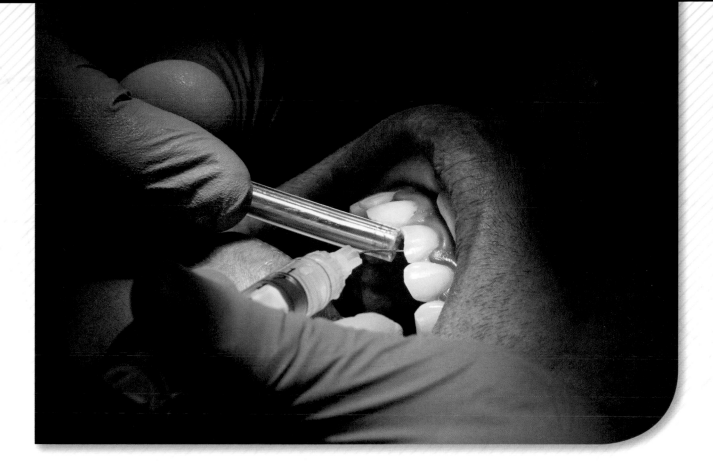

of the US population is at least somewhat fearful of dental procedures, and 10 to 15 percent say they are extremely fearful.[5] Concern for patients' dental pain phobias stems back to the mid-1900s, when techniques were developed to be more considerate of the patient.

In 1945, Niels Bjorn Jorgensen consulted with Dr. Forrest Leffingwell at Loma Linda University in California to develop a technique to minimize patient fear. This groundbreaking method of anesthesia,

Balanced Anesthesia

In 1926, John Lundy of the Mayo Clinic in Minnesota introduced a method for administering anesthesia called balanced anesthesia. This method combines a mix of anesthetic drugs to achieve a desired effect, such as nitrous oxide for anxiety relief, a local anesthetic for pain relief, and a general anesthetic for overall sedation. Balanced anesthesia has its advantages. First, balanced anesthesia allows doctors to administer lesser amounts of multiple anesthetics, rather than a high dosage of a single drug. This helps increase safety by reducing the amounts of each drug and thereby reducing the chance of toxicity in the patient. The lower doses of each drug result in less stress on organs plus a faster recovery.

Since the early 1900s, balanced anesthesia has evolved to combine even more agents, such as analgesics, sedatives, and muscle relaxants. Technically, if an anesthesiologist mixes two agents together, he or she is using a balanced anesthesia technique.

now known worldwide as the Jorgensen technique, combines multiple anesthetic agents to strike a balance between pain relief and sedation. With careful timing and placement of the local anesthetic agents, the Jorgensen technique provides adequate levels of sedation and pain relief while remaining quite safe. The still-conscious but mildly sedated patients keep their reflexes intact, and their breathing and heart rate remain normal. This allows the practitioner to work and still communicate with a conscious patient.

Today, the most common drug used for anxiety control is nitrous oxide. It is used by more than half of all dentists in the United States.[7] While it is not one of the Jorgensen drugs, the method of combining anxiety and pain relief in dentistry marks an important step in anesthesia.

Local Anesthetics and Obstetrics

Obstetric anesthesia has been rooted in controversy from its earliest use. Proponents of anesthesia praised its contribution to pain-free births. However, some opponents saw it as a "dangerous folly."[8] Stemming from their Christian religious beliefs, many believed childbirth was a "reminder of Eve's original sin in the garden of Eden," so they thought it was sinful if a woman did not feel the pain of childbirth.[9] It was a natural phenomenon, they argued, and nature should not be interfered with.

Today, one of the major choices a mother-to-be faces is whether to have a natural childbirth without medication or receive a form of analgesia. Proponents of natural childbirth advocate for a medication-free birth, saying it is safer. Others believe a woman has the right to be free of pain. They declare modern techniques are indeed safe and time-tested. Regardless of what a woman decides, she always has the option of pain relief.

Popular forms of regional anesthesia include an epidural, spinal, or combined spinal-epidural (CSE). These techniques allow the woman to remain alert and awake. An epidural is so named because the thin hollow needle and catheter—which carries the anesthetic—is inserted into what is called the epidural space in the spine in the lower back. It allows the mother to cooperate and actively participate during the labor process while the drug is administered as needed during labor.

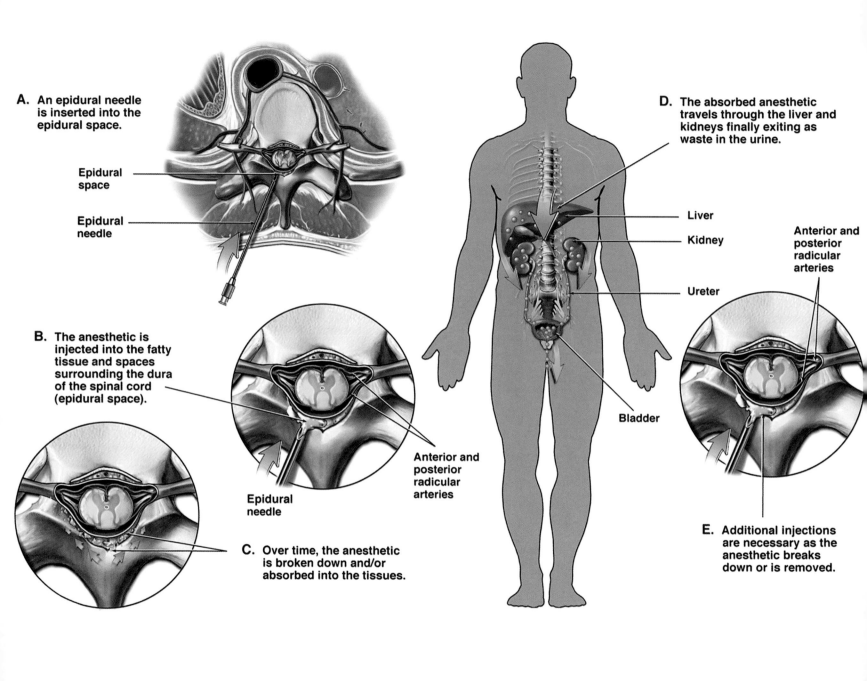

A. An epidural needle is inserted into the epidural space.

Epidural space

Epidural needle

B. The anesthetic is injected into the fatty tissue and spaces surrounding the dura of the spinal cord (epidural space).

C. Over time, the anesthetic is broken down and/or absorbed into the tissues.

Epidural needle

Anterior and posterior radicular arteries

D. The absorbed anesthetic travels through the liver and kidneys finally exiting as waste in the urine.

Liver

Kidney

Ureter

Bladder

Anterior and posterior radicular arteries

E. Additional injections are necessary as the anesthetic breaks down or is removed.

With spinal analgesia, a smaller needle is inserted deeper into the spinal fluid in a single procedure that delivers all the medication at once. The CSE combines an initial injection of anesthetic fluid followed by a catheter for a controlled release of a drug. The CSE acts 15 to 20 minutes quicker than a standard epidural, making it popular for traditional and Cesarean deliveries.[10] Several factors, including the condition of the woman and the fetus and the availability of qualified staff and equipment, are taken into consideration before deciding upon an epidural, spinal analgesia, or in some cases general anesthesia.

A Cesarean delivery is a major surgical process. The unborn child is removed from the uterus surgically by an incision made in the front of the mother's body. However, epidurals and spinal anesthesia are typically used during Cesareans to give the mother an option to be aware rather than asleep with a general anesthetic.

 An epidural anesthetic is injected directly into the epidural space in the spine.

Pain-Free and Relaxed

The throb of headaches, sharpness of lower back pain, burn of neuropathy, and tender pain of fibromyalgia: these are examples of chronic pain syndromes suffered by millions of people throughout the world. Pain itself is the most prevalent type of suffering and disability, as well as the most frequent reason people seek medical treatment. Chronic pain disables and reduces the quality of life, thus making pain management and relief the most common anesthetic treatment.

From toothaches to headaches, everyone has experienced the onset of some type of pain. It is a great motivator, driving us to find relief by any means. But it is also a hindrance, sometimes severe enough that it interferes with our daily lives. Today's society values pain relief as a proper way to

Since the advent of anesthetics, people have come to expect relief from chronic and occasional pain.

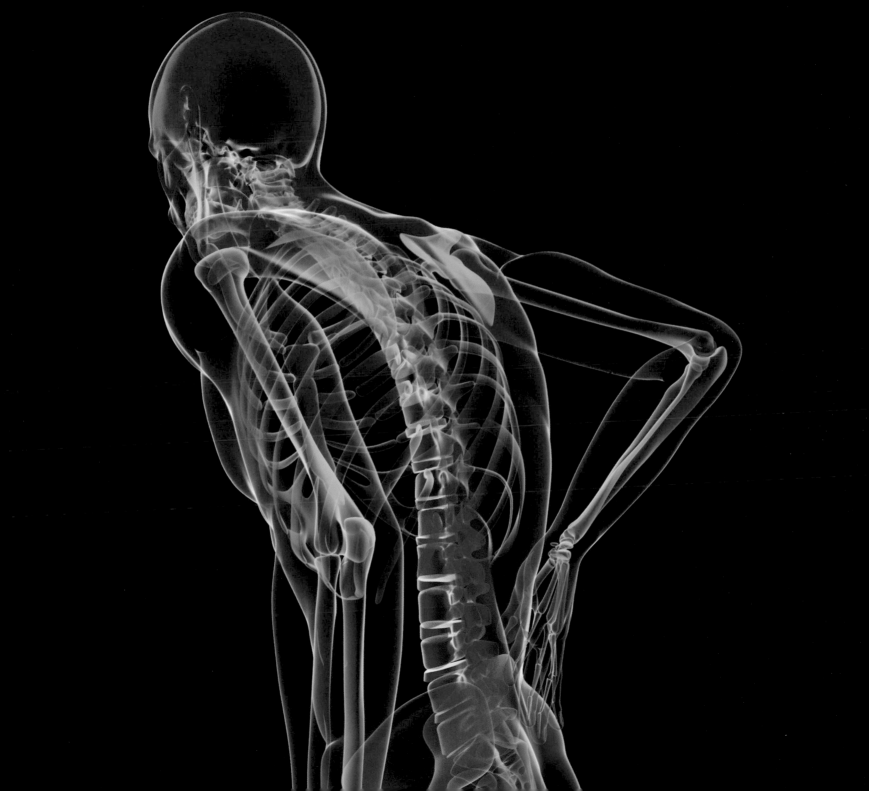

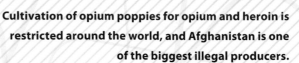

Cultivation of opium poppies for opium and heroin is restricted around the world, and Afghanistan is one of the biggest illegal producers.

Fibromyalgia is a combination of conditions that consist of chronic widespread pain. This condition carries with it other symptoms, such as fatigue, stiff muscle joints, and sleep disorders. Despite widespread usage, anti-inflammatory drugs and opioids are not effective treatments for fibromyalgia.

live, as a right. There is a type of pain relief for any ailment, from aspirin for a headache to a prescribed medication for post-surgery relief.

Opioids

One of the oldest types of analgesics is a group of compounds called opioids—also known as narcotics. Cultivation of the opium poppy, from which opioids are derived, dates back as far as 3400 BCE in Mesopotamia. The plant's milky juice was taken for pain relief. However, people also used opium for pleasure because it caused relaxation and a dreamy state, even though the drug is highly physically addicting. By the 1800s, the global trade in opium was so valuable it was a factor in two wars between the British and the Chinese.

In 1805, German pharmacist Friedrich Wilhelm Adam Sertürner isolated the chemicals in opium. He recognized the potency of opium's active ingredient, the chemical compound morphine. Morphine came into widespread use in the 1800s—some even said it was a cure for opium addition—but doctors

gradually recognized its potential for addiction. By the early 1900s it was more tightly regulated, as was opium.

In 1874, C. R. Wright, an English medical researcher, boiled morphine and was left with a new drug, heroin. Heroin was first sold as a miracle drug and a nonaddictive cure for morphine addiction. It is faster acting and stronger than morphine. However, as with morphine, doctors soon realized heroin is highly addictive. Today, heroin is illegal in the United States, while morphine use is allowed only with a doctor's prescription.

Opium, morphine, heroin, and chemically similar drugs are called opioids because they stimulate the body's opioid receptors. There are three receptors, each indicated by a Greek letter name: Mu, Delta, and Kappa. Opioid receptors are found on nerves throughout the brain, spinal cord, digestive tract, and other areas. The goal of opioid use is to produce analgesia and maintain stable blood flow during anesthesia. They can raise a person's pain threshold, which in turn reduces the intensity of pain.

Common types of opioids include morphine, codeine, diamorphine, pethidine, fentanyl, sufentanil, and remifentanil. Side effects can include lowered breathing

✛ Drug-Free Pain Relief— Ice It

When you have a sprained thumb or toe, or have hurt your elbow, simply ice it. Called cryotherapy, this common remedy for minor sports injuries is another effective way to relieve pain. Ice constricts the blood vessels, reducing the flow of blood to the injured area. This in turn reduces nerve activity. The result is temporary dulling of pain and relief for many ailments, such as toothaches, bruises, and itching.

Morphine Effects from Snake Venom

Mambalgins are proteins found in the venom of the black mamba. The snake's venom is one of the most poisonous in the world. The venom can kill a mammal quickly with its nerve poison, causing loss of muscle control, mental functions, and sensation. Recent studies have shown, however, that isolated mambalgins provide an analgesic effect similar to that of morphine. Mice test subjects developed a dependence on the drug similar to morphine dependence, but it was less severe than a morphine addiction and it did not cause breathing complications. Testing has yet to begin on humans, but scientists are optimistic about its effects as a pain reliever.

Nature's Muscle Relaxant

Curare is a poison produced from the bark of the *Chondrodendron tomentosum* vine, which grows in the treetop canopies in South America's tropical rain forests. South American indigenous tribes have utilized the natural muscle relaxer as an effective tool in hunting game. They spread the gumlike curare paste on the tips of their arrows, and animals they shoot become paralyzed. Western knowledge of its effects dates back to 1595, when Sir Walter Raleigh encountered inhabitants of the Amazon rain forest who used it. British interest in the drug began in the 1700s, resulting in numerous expeditions in the Amazon and research about the plant. In 1856, Claude Bernard discovered how the drug effects the body's nerves and muscles. In 1938, Richard and Ruth Gill led an expedition to gather 25 pounds (11 kg) of curare paste for processing into neuromuscular blocking drugs that cause relaxation and temporary paralysis.[1]

rate, constipation, sedation, drug dependence, and nausea and vomiting.

The US Drug Enforcement Administration (DEA) classifies opioids into five schedules that define whether they have a medical use and what their abuse potential is. Opioids listed on schedules two through five indicate they are appropriate for medical use, although they have varying potential for addiction. These include such drugs as hydrocodone (brand name Vicodin), oxycodone (brand name Oxycontin), codeine (often used in cough suppressants), and anabolic steroids. Schedule one drugs, such as heroin, are not used medically, and they carry a high addiction potential.

NSAIDs and Non-Opioids

Inflammation sometimes accompanies painful conditions. Finding treatment for inflammation—including fevers—dates back thousands of years. Hippocrates, a Greek physician who lived in the 400s BCE, used an extract from willow bark and leaves called willow bark salicin. The German company Kolbe began producing salicylic acid in 1860. Soon, drug company Bayer began producing the form we now know as aspirin in 1899. All of these are what are referred to as nonsteroidal anti-inflammatory drugs, or NSAIDs (pronounced EHN-sayds).

These types of drugs—also called nonnarcotic or non-opioid—have weak analgesic effects. They are used to relieve mild pain in addition to lowering inflammation. They do not have the drawback of opioids' many side effects. In some cases, they are effective post-surgery pain relievers and can be used together with opioids.

Inflammation is triggered by an enzyme known as cyclooxygenase (COX). COX comes in two forms, COX-1 and COX-2. This enzyme also helps protect the stomach lining and aids with kidney functions. NSAIDs such as aspirin, ibuprofen, and naproxen prevent this enzyme from working, which is why, in addition to relieving pain and inflammation, they also can upset your stomach.

6

Anesthesia Techniques and Technology

Anesthetic drugs must be administered properly or they will be less effective. One of the most important things a doctor can do is the preoperative evaluation, in which a patient's medical history and general health are reviewed. The result of the evaluation determines the best method to use. Choosing the right technique helps reduce the likelihood of complications during or after anesthesia. Trained specialists deliver general anesthesia using sophisticated anesthesia machines. Or they perform specialized nerve blocks designed to keep the patient alert but without sensation during surgery. Whatever the type of anesthesia, patients' vital signs are monitored to ensure safety.

Surgeons and anesthesiologists must consult about their patients before surgery.

✚ Anesthesiologists

Anesthesiologists are doctors who specialize in providing anesthesia to patients undergoing varying forms of medical procedures. Anesthesiologists manage the unconscious, protect vital organs under anesthetic stress, relieve pain, evaluate their patients before and after a procedure, and advise other doctors on anesthetic delivery. Certification as an anesthesiologist requires four additional years of postgraduate study after the doctor of medicine or osteopathy degree has been obtained. There are many national and international organizations dedicated to this important medical specialty.

Preparation and Evaluation

A person has decided to have surgery. His or her doctor has explained the procedure, and as part of the surgery preparation, the patient is referred to an anesthesiologist. This is the specialist who will be responsible for administering anesthesia during the surgery. Not only does the patient want to be informed of all the procedures, but the anesthesiologist needs to know the patient, too. This is part of preparing for anesthesia, long before the first drug is ever administered.

The anesthesiologist wants to know the patient and understand him or her from a medical point of view. The patient's medical history is reviewed, and any existing conditions such as obesity or poor nutrition are evaluated. Does the patient have diabetes, poor circulation, or respiratory problems? Is the patient on any medications? The anesthesiologist takes all of this into account to determine the best types of drugs for the procedure.

The specialist asks if the patient has any reservations about general anesthesia—the "going to sleep" aspect of it. Is the patient anxious? If so, the specialist can schedule a pre-anesthesia sedative. Presurgery anxiety is common with children, and sometimes nitrous oxide is used to help calm anxiety.

It may be determined the patient will require some form of sedative to help him or her relax before receiving the anesthetic agents. Pre-medication techniques are designed for that purpose. Sedatives help patients relax by decreasing their metabolism. Because of this, they also reduce the amount of the regular anesthetic dose required. The anesthesiologist might give an orally administered barbiturate or narcotic. In this case, however, the specialist chooses nitrous oxide.

Now that the patient has been evaluated, the anesthesiologist finds out about the particulars of the surgery. Knowing these details and keeping a good working relationship with the surgeons is important. It helps the anesthesiologist anticipate any pain or other complications that might arise.

Day of Surgery

The patient arrives. He or she knows the procedure and has given consent. The anesthesiologist checks the anesthesia machine and makes sure its parts and functions are in working order, including all masks, tubes, probes, suctions, and ventilators. The monitors are checked and the drugs and their appropriate doses are assembled. The surgeons are ready.

In the operating room, the anesthesiologist affixes a mask to the patient's nose and begins administering nitrous oxide. Within minutes, the patient is relaxed but still able to talk. Next, the anesthesiologist inserts an IV tube into the patient's arm. Within that same minute, the patient begins receiving an IV agent such as propofol. The patient loses consciousness before he or she realizes it. At this time, the nitrous oxide is switched off and replaced with oxygen. This reduces the chance of hypoxia (lack of oxygen) during anesthesia care before doctors insert the patient's breathing tube.

The anesthesiologist gives a second agent, a neuromuscular blocking drug, to relax throat muscles. Neuromuscular blocking drugs affect the nerves and muscles to cause relaxation and temporary paralysis. This helps the anesthesiologist insert the breathing tube. The patient has been successfully anesthetized with a nitrous oxide sedative, IV propofol, and a neuromuscular blocking drug. This technique is then combined with an inhalation anesthetic (either isoflurane, sevoflurane, or desflurane) along with an opioid (usually fentanyl or remifentanil) to provide ongoing balanced anesthesia. In some instances when inhalational anesthetics need to be avoided, IV propofol is used to keep the patient anesthetized.

Anesthesia for surgery often includes multiple agents given through a mask and an IV.

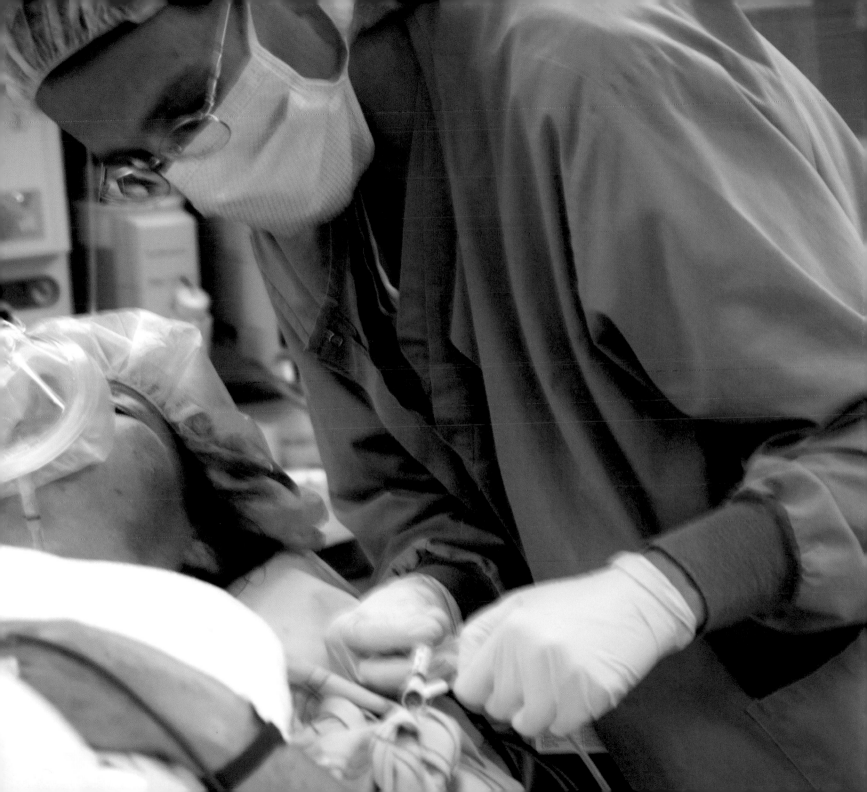

Modern anesthesia machines can monitor vital signs
and administer anesthetics precisely, but a trained
anesthesiologist is still necessary.

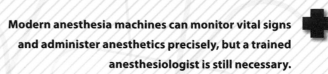

Anesthesia Machines

If the patient is induced by means of an inhaled agent, such as sevoflurane, an anesthesia machine delivers the gas and monitors the patient. Today's anesthesia workstations are complex, computer-controlled devices that have a breathing system attached. These machines are designed specifically for anesthetic gases. They control the amount of anesthetic gases and oxygen administered to the patient. If the oxygen supply fails, an alarm will sound and the machine will shut off so the patient does not receive anesthetic gases without the proper mix of oxygen.

Proper monitoring ensures a safe procedure. Monitors attached to the anesthetic machine show changes in the physiology of a patient, allowing specialists to respond accordingly. The types of measurements made in monitoring include, but are not limited to, blood pressure, heartbeat, body temperature, brain activity, and oxygen and anesthetic levels in the blood. They also monitor the carbon dioxide the patient breaths out. The monitors show how the anesthetic equipment is working and also how the patient is responding to the drugs. They are equipped with alarm systems to alert doctors if apnea (loss of breathing) occurs or if something becomes disconnected in the breathing circuit. More important than any monitor, however, is an attentive anesthesiologist who can interpret the data to make decisions.

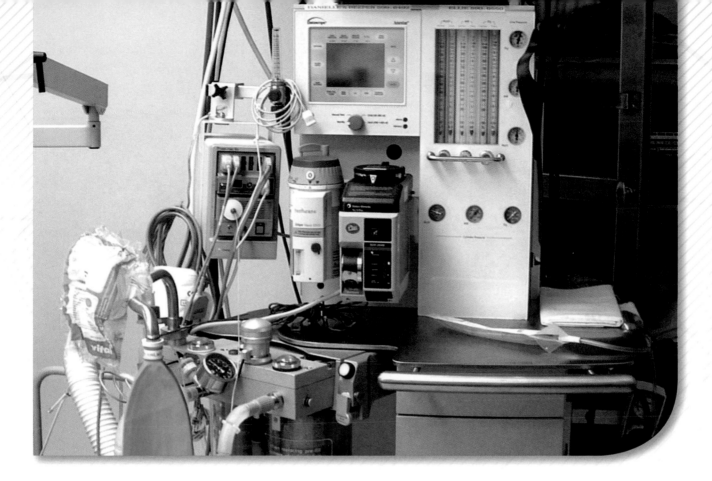

Regional Anesthesia

The hypothetical "patient" now requires surgery on his or her leg but does not need to go to sleep for it. In fact, the patient does not want to. This is when regional anesthesia is used. A regional anesthesia

Animal Anesthesia

Similar to humans, animals undergoing painful medical procedures must receive a balanced anesthesia approach of sedation, analgesia, amnesia, and unconsciousness. Reducing anxiety, especially in dogs and cats, is important because the stress can be just as uncomfortable as pain. For the most part, the preoperative assessment and choice of anesthetic drugs is similar to humans. Some specific factors are considered, however, such as the breed of animal, its temperament, and the procedure.

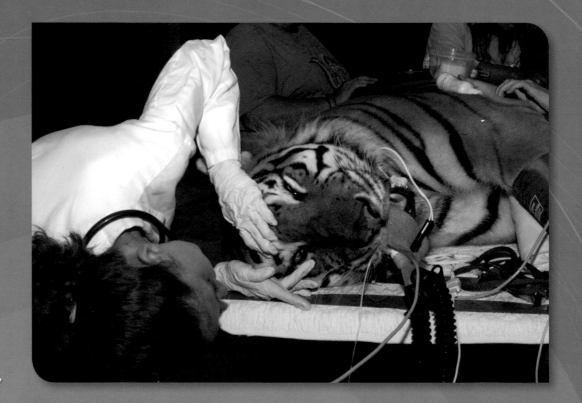

patient retains consciousness but does not feel the surgery happening. In this case, the hypothetical patient is undergoing a specialized technique—a peripheral nerve block.

Peripheral nerves make up the peripheral nervous system. These are the sets of nerves that connect the limbs and organs to the central nervous system. Peripheral nerve blocks are a form of regional anesthesia. They are used for surgeries, diagnosing pain, and postoperative pain relief. This method is designed to block off sets of nerves, preventing sensations to specific regions of the body. Patients are still evaluated as if they were receiving general anesthesia, and they may receive supplemental sedation if they are uncomfortable during surgery.

There are more than a dozen major types of nerve block techniques, each designed to block nerve receptors to the extremities, including arms, fingers, feet, toes, and organs—to name just a few. Blocking techniques given to larger nerves can block off sensation to the entire arm or leg, while more localized blocking of peripheral nerves can anesthetize smaller sections, such as a hand or foot.

To perform a peripheral nerve block, a specialist must first locate the nerve. Specialists used to prick the skin to

+ Monitored Anesthesia

Monitored anesthesia care is best defined as a level of anesthesia that is not general anesthesia (when the patient is completely asleep) or local anesthesia (when the patient is wide awake). It is also known as conscious sedation, although the term is incorrect. It is used for surgical procedures that do not require deep sedation or general anesthesia. Under monitored anesthesia care, the patient continues breathing normally. In addition, the patient is able to respond to commands, which can make surgeries go more smoothly.

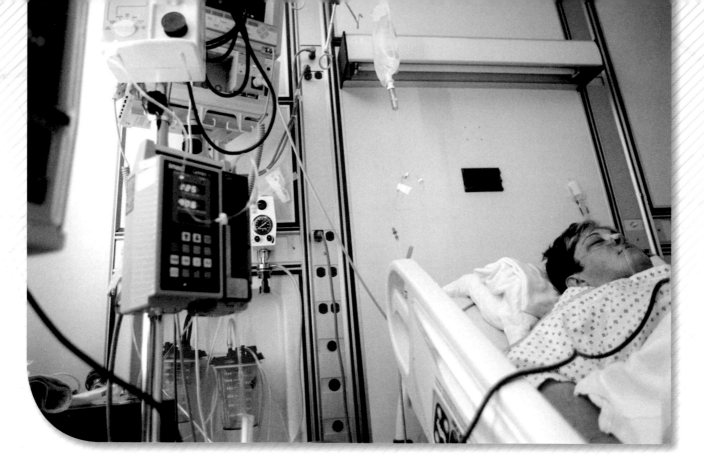

find the nerve. This carried considerable risks: it was possible to cause irreversible nerve damage. Today, nerve stimulators reduce the potential for this traumatic nerve damage. Through a needle, the nerve stimulator delivers an electric current to the nerves, making the muscles move. It is not always accurate on the first try, and often the needle and current need to be adjusted to locate the correct nerve. Along with nerve stimulators, bedside ultrasound devices are used to guide the needle close to the nerves that

After surgery, patients must be monitored while they awaken. Many require morphine or another pain reliever for post-surgery pain.

are to be blocked. This improves the precision and success rate of the block. Once a specialist locates the nerve, he or she inserts a hollow syringe needle. Then a catheter is inserted through the hollow needle so the anesthetic can be injected into the body.

Post-Anesthesia Recovery

The surgery is complete. The patient is in the recovery room, gradually beginning to awaken from the surgery. As patients transition from an anesthetized state, their circulation, ventilation, and oxygenation are still being monitored.

It is in the early recovery stages that the patient is most likely to suffer from anesthetic side effects. Nausea and vomiting, airway obstruction, and high blood pressure are frequently encountered after surgery. Other effects can include delirium, shivering due to lowered body temperature, and delayed awakening. An anesthetic is only as good as the technique used to deliver it, the informed specialist delivering the drug, and the monitoring system used to safely bring the patient in and out of anesthesia.

Issues in Anesthesia

Despite state-of-the-art equipment and trained staff, anesthesia still carries a variety of risks, mostly because each patient has a unique response to anesthetics. Each person's body and medical history is different, and a particular anesthetic agent or technique that works safely for one person may make another person sick. Disease, old age, pregnancy, and youth are all big factors to consider when preparing an anesthetic treatment. Critical care, trauma, and postoperative pain are special circumstances that also carry their own set of issues.

Although anesthesiologists take careful measures to ensure the safety of each patient, the drugs themselves are in fact very dangerous. They are toxic and can be deadly if used improperly. Without strict regulation and careful administration, evaluation, and monitoring, a commonly used dose can

Doctors must consider the effects anesthesia, analgesics, and other medications can have on a fetus when prescribed during a woman's pregnancy.

Intensive Care and Trauma

Trauma, or life-threatening injuries, require an anesthesiologist as a critical member of the trauma team unit. Injuries to the head, brain, chest, spine, or internal organs, as well as severe burns, constitute many of the major traumatic-type injuries. Because of the severity of these injuries, general anesthetics are the drug of choice. Anesthesia administration is trickier in these cases, as a patient who experienced an accident has not been prepared for surgery, and his or her medical history is unknown.

easily become a lethal dose. It is a thin line. Patients with problematic lung or heart functions, trauma victims, or heart surgery patients must receive smaller doses. Existing health conditions, age, and pregnancy are additional factors.

Diseases

Doctors must determine whether the patient suffers from any diseases or conditions that might affect the surgery or anesthetics. Such conditions might require a different mix of anesthetic drugs or special monitoring during anesthesia.

Cardiovascular disease is the leading cause of death in the United States and Europe. There are many types of heart disease, and patients receiving anesthesia who also have heart disease are at a higher risk for complications. Diseases that cause difficulty in breathing, such as sleep apnea, asthma, emphysema, and bronchitis, pose great risks as well. These types of conditions require specialists to monitor how the patient's lungs are working. Patients may require drugs in addition to the anesthetic agents to help with airflow blockage or inflammation in the lungs.

The kidneys and liver can cause additional complications. The liver metabolizes and detoxifies drugs, absorbs nutrients, and produces essential proteins for the body. Its function affects almost every organ in the body. The kidneys act as a filter as they excrete drugs. Maintaining blood flow and kidney function is crucial during anesthesia. Not doing so may result in kidney failure. Advanced age, preexisting kidney disease, and heart failure all contribute to a greater likelihood of kidney failure.

Obesity

Obesity and malnutrition can cause other anesthesia complications. Approximately one-third of the US adult population is classified as obese. When patients carry excess weight, they need to consume more air to support their bodies. This can cause a higher rate of breathing. Inserting a breathing tube into the throat may become more difficult. In addition, body positioning and accessing the surgical area can present a challenge. Drugs can respond differently due to the extra amount of fatty tissues in the body, so anesthesiologists sometimes have to adjust dosages or choose different drugs.

Physician Aid-in-Dying

Euthanasia—a doctor directly ending a patient's life—is illegal in the United States. However, physician aid-in-dying is legal in Washington, Oregon, and Montana. In physician aid-in-dying, a doctor provides medicines to the patient that the patient takes herself. Often the medication is a painkiller given in such a dose that it will kill the patient while relieving the pain. Or a patient can take sedatives as death draws near. Withholding treatment to a terminally ill patient at his or her request is legal throughout the country.

Physician aid-in-dying presents many ethical issues. On the one hand, it is compassionate to help people end their lives if they are suffering, and physician aid-in-dying allows patients to make their own medical decisions. On the other hand, society generally believes in preserving life at any cost. In addition, doctors can make mistakes, and some worry patients who could live might end their lives based on a mistaken assessment of their chances. Also, some worry patients might be pressured into ending their lives because of the cost of continuing care.

Elderly Patients

When a human ages, his or her organs stop performing at their highest level. The body loses muscle mass and gains body fat. In the central nervous system, there is a loss of nerve tissue. Digestion in the intestines slows due to the decrease in the body's levels of the chemical serotonin. The brain loses some of its ability to feel pleasure, as levels of the chemical dopamine also drop. This affects memory, reasoning, and perception. The respiratory muscles weaken, and liver and kidney tissue mass decreases, affecting metabolism. This aging can vary by environment, diet, and genetics.

Most often, the elderly need smaller doses of anesthetics. Inhaled drugs act quicker, and recovery takes longer. As with inhaled agents, IV agents also increase in potency and last longer in the elderly.

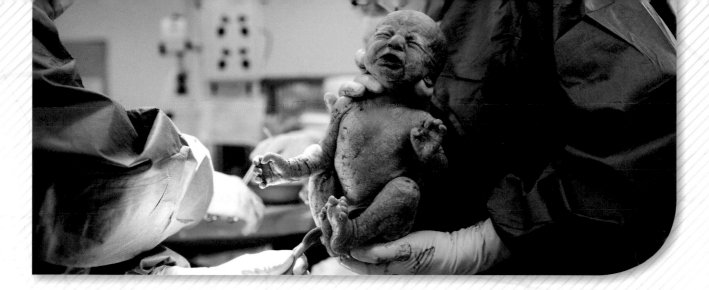

Humane anesthetic use becomes critical at the end of life, when death is inevitable but doctors can still ease the patient's passing. In hospice care, doctors continue to medicate the symptoms of disease, including pain, even as they are no longer attempting to stop death. Pain relief is a critical component in supporting the patient.

Pediatrics

Children, particularly infants, are at a higher risk than adults for complications from anesthesia. Organs are still growing. The kidneys are still developing their abilities to filter and cleanse. Infants have a higher risk of breathing complications. The air sacs in the lungs are multiplying, and the diaphragm and the rib cage that hold everything in place are still growing, too. Managing an infant's small airway requires precise equipment, perfect technique, and close monitoring. During anesthesia, specialists face special challenges in managing fluid and mineral loss in infants.

According to a 2012 article published in the journal *Pediatrics*, children who received general anesthesia before age three showed higher signs of language and memory problems later in life. The study is based on a sample size of more than 2,600 children, in which 321 were exposed to anesthesia before age three and the rest were not.[1] Therapy soon after anesthesia use may help reduce or reverse this effect.

Obstetrics

During pregnancy, a woman's body goes through hormonal and other physical changes. Blood production and flow increases, but blood pressure drops. Her minute ventilation (the volume of air inhaled and exhaled per minute) increases, though lung capacity decreases. Nervous system changes increase the potency of inhaled anesthetics.

Another complication during pregnancy arises when anesthetics enter the placenta, which nurtures the fetus. The fetus can suffer developmentally depending on how much of the anesthetics pass through the placenta and enter the fetus. This is particularly dangerous during the first trimester of pregnancy.

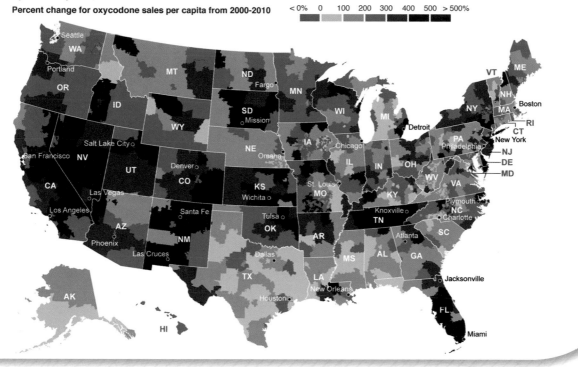

Painkiller nation: prescription sales boom across U.S. from 2000 to 2010

Sales of the nation's two most popular prescription painkillers, oxycodone and hydrocodone, have exploded across the U.S. in the last decade, according to an Associated Press analysis of data provided by the Drug Enforcement Administration. This map shows increases in per-capita sales of oxycodone, the key ingredient in OxyContin, Percocet and Percodan.

Percent change for oxycodone sales per capita from 2000-2010   < 0% 0   100 200 300 400 500 > 500%

Addiction Risk

Derivatives of morphine, such as hydrocodone (Vicodin) and oxycodone (Oxycontin), are common analgesics prescribed to relive postoperative pain. Despite their effectiveness, patients can develop a tolerance to the drugs, needing more to attain the same effect. This can ultimately result in dependence.

Opiate addiction is a growing problem in the United States, with an estimated 1.4 million people addicted to painkillers. This is separate from the additional 1 million users of the illegal narcotic heroin.[2] The body's dependence grows strong enough that it can make breaking the habit require additional medication. The synthetic opioid methadone was first used to stop these addictions in the 1960s. Naltrexone was introduced in the 1980s, though it is not commonly used today. Buprenorphine is the drug developed most recently to combat the effects of opiate abuse. It can decrease symptoms of withdrawal. These medications are prescribed together with counseling to help patients break their addiction.

Anesthesia Awareness

Patients under anesthesia are monitored carefully with complex anesthesia machines. The gas amounts are controlled and precise. The vital signs are detailed and constant. But for all of this monitoring, control, and safety, there is still the risk of anesthesia awareness. This problem touches on the fear of surgery, as patients worry about the horrific possibility of waking up during a surgery.

Approximately one to two patients out of every 1,000 experience anesthesia awareness during surgery.[3] The most common cause of awareness is simply that the patient did not receive an adequate level of anesthesia or the required dose was not well tolerated. Sometimes, the patient requires more anesthesia than initially calculated. Occasionally the equipment used in monitoring malfunctions, but this is less common. Some patients don't seem to gain awareness during the surgery, but after, they spontaneously recollect events that occurred during the operation. Patients can even develop post-traumatic stress disorder as a result.

While anesthesia researchers are studying methods to completely guarantee patients will remain unaware, a solution is far from found. Scientists are studying consciousness and what it means to be awake, but these states of awareness are not well understood. To help prevent patients from becoming aware during their surgery, or remember it later, better anesthesia monitors are needed to measure the levels of the patient's anesthesia. Additionally, better administration of drugs and using proper combinations of anesthetic agents will also help.

Organ Transplants

General anesthesia is used in all organ transplant procedures. An anesthesiologist's role might include caring for patients who have already received transplants, prospective organ recipients, and living and cadaver organ donors. Ethics become an issue as well, as cadaveric donors must be certified brain-dead before a procedure takes place. It is often the specialist's role to determine this, as well as to take care of the organ and its preservation until it is implanted.

Ethical Considerations

Using anesthetics is dangerous and can cause permanent damage or death. The doctors, patients, and family members involved must decide if the risk of not acting and not performing the surgery is greater than the risk of undergoing anesthesia and surgery.

In most cases, the patient must give what is called "informed consent." Standards determining how much the doctor must tell the patient vary by location. Generally the doctor must give the patient enough information that an average patient would be able to make a decision based on the facts of the

Elderly patients with dementia may not be able to give informed consent for their own medical procedures.

situation. The discussion should include "common risks even if they are not serious, and very serious risks, such as death, even if they are not common."[4]

However, the situation becomes more complicated if the patient is not able to participate in making the decision, for example if she does not understand where she is or what is happening. In many such cases, a family member or other legal substitute then makes the decision. In emergencies, doctors can usually assume consent if the patient cannot consent and there is no family member or legal substitute available.

Do Not Resuscitate

For reasons that can include age or incurable illness, some hospital patients have "do not resuscitate" (DNR) orders in place. This means medical staff members are instructed not to perform cardiopulmonary resuscitation (CPR) or take similar actions to keep the patient alive in the event of heart failure. A DNR order can cause an ethical dilemma for an anesthesiologist because routine anesthesia care involves many of the same actions as CPR. When are the anesthesiologist's actions routine, and when do they become the type of extreme methods not allowed under a DNR order? Ideally, the patient and doctor discuss before the surgery possible scenarios and what procedures the patient would not like to undergo in an extreme situation. Therefore the DNR order may be lifted temporarily while the patient is under anesthesia care. It is important for the anesthesiologist and other doctors to obey the patient's wishes (or the family's wishes) when they are known.

8

Advancements and the Future

In just the past 50 years, anesthesia techniques, equipment, and drugs have advanced rapidly, making surgery safer and allowing surgeons to perform procedures that would have once been too risky. In the 1840s, the first widely used anesthetics were ether, chloroform, and nitrous oxide. They were all important in their own right, and nitrous oxide continues to be used today. The greatest advancements of the 1900s came with the introduction of new anesthetic agents.

In the 1950s, flammable gases were phased out, replaced with safer and less flammable halogenated gases. These gases, including sevoflurane and desflurane, worked quickly and wore off quickly. As the decades passed, even more potent gases were introduced. Intravenous local anesthetic agents, neuromuscular blocking drugs, opioid analgesics, and anti-inflammatory drugs

Anesthesiologists can now refine their skills using dummies that react to anesthesia and other drugs.

became new ways to block pain and help improve anesthesia quality of care. Several options are also available to minimize nausea and vomiting.

The invention of local anesthetics and opioid analgesics allowed doctors to master new approaches in regional anesthesia. Epidurals, spinal anesthesia, and peripheral nerve blocking gave doctors the ability to target specific areas of the body. As new methods developed, so did the technology. Computerized anesthesia machines that deliver inhaled anesthetics have become standard equipment.

The future and advancement of anesthesiology leans heavily toward the development of new technology. This could mean new drug development and testing to produce safer drugs. A newer and safer agent, xenon, is in the works. New technologies that allow for less invasive preoperation testing or genetic profiling of patients to tailor drug selection are under investigation.

New Drugs and Safety

Improving anesthesia largely depends on modifying existing drugs rather than developing new ones. One way researchers are looking to curb the dangers of anesthesia is by tailoring drugs specifically to each component of anesthesia: sedation, immobility, analgesia, and amnesia. By studying how anesthetics affect each of these components, they can determine which nerve points produce these separate effects. Body and brain scans are beginning to clarify researchers' understanding of

Hot Peppers and Pain

Capsaicin, the chemical in hot peppers that gives you a burning sensation, has been proven to be an analgesic. It is commonly used as an additive in over-the-counter topical creams that help relieve muscle and joint pain. When applied directly to a wound, however, it provides the same burning sensation as when applied to the tongue. This may feel good on sore muscles, but it isn't recommended for open wounds. Researchers, however, have tested it as an additive to local anesthetic treatments. They combined it with QX-314—a derivative of lidocaine—for dental procedures. Capsaicin dulls the pain receptors but does not affect the neurons that affect other sensations, such as motor function. Scientists are working to neutralize the initial burn of capsaicin before it can be effectively injected on its own.

Video Games as Pain Relief?

Scientists have experimented with using multimedia such as video games and television to help distract children from pain. The theory behind this method is to divert attention away from the stimulus, leaving the patient to focus on other stimuli, reducing the perception and experience of pain. This theory has led to the use of virtual reality as pain distraction. Patients "immerse" themselves into the computer reality and feel they are actually in the environment. Using virtual reality to distract from pain was first attempted on two adolescent burn patients.[2] Both reported less pain. Experiments were also performed on adults, who also reported reduction in pain. However, the sample sizes for testing were small and not diverse, and it has only been tested on a few types of pain situations. Research continues to broaden the treatment's applications.

anesthesia's effects on the brain, spinal cord, and other related body structures. As researcher Beverley A. Orser explains, "With a cocktail of compounds, each of which produces only one desirable end point, the future version of anesthesia care could leave a patient conversant but pain-free while having a broken limb repaired or immobile and sedated but aware while having a hip replaced."[1]

The development of new drugs always takes into consideration a balance of characteristics: potency, safety, and rapid elimination that allows for a rapid recovery. When sevoflurane was introduced, it was safer and worked more quickly than its predecessor, halothane. The most recent gas, desflurane, is even safer and just as potent, and it is eliminated more quickly so patients recover faster. These characteristics make it popular for surgeries that do not require an overnight stay.

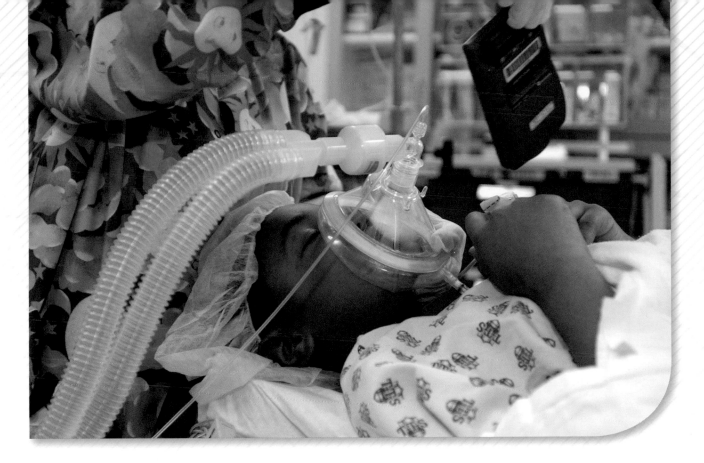

Currently, researchers are altering the molecular structure of existing drugs to create better ones. The goal is "fast, clean, and soft" drug development, meaning speedy development (fast) with predictable effects (soft) and without unwanted side effects (clean). One of these new drugs is an update of the IV drug etomidate, which is a short-acting sedative.

One of the ways researchers are altering drugs is by using computer simulations to test their effects. Remimazolam is being tested with computer models to help it onset quicker, which scientists say can help doctors tailor the doses better.

Xenon is a noble gas on the periodic table, and in 1939 its anesthetic properties were discovered. Xenon has many of the characteristics of an ideal inhalational agent. It is odorless and nontoxic, it does not catch fire, and it is stable under normal air pressure. The only problem with xenon is its cost. It is a rare element and requires much energy to extract and prepare it for use. New technology is being developed to produce xenon more cheaply. Researchers are developing a system to recycle the gas.

Technology

The ability to deliver continuous electronic monitoring is at the core of anesthesia safety, and new technology brings continual improvements. Closed-loop anesthesia systems administer a balanced mixture of anesthetic agents and oxygen to the patient. New technology is being developed to further control the gas delivery and also analyze the depth of a patient's sedation and overall anesthesia. These developments can help better regulate the mixtures, eventually allowing the computer system to monitor and maintain the proper dosage levels at all times.

While developing newer, more automated closed-loop systems can seem cutting-edge and necessary, the need for highly trained anesthesiologists still takes precedence. New technology cannot replace a skilled specialist who understands the patient and the surgery and can tailor anesthesia accordingly. Closed-loop systems, however, can assist in more mundane tasks of anesthesia, making multiple adjustments per minute to stabilize the depth of anesthesia and regulate body fluids.

Nanotechnology

A nanometer is one-billionth of a meter, a microscopic unit of measure used in the research of nanotechnology. This concept of nanotechnology was introduced by physicist and Nobel Laureate Richard Feynman in 1959 and has been applied to use in medicine. Uses of this technology in medicine include disease diagnosis, molecular

+ Suspended Animation

Hydrogen sulfide, commonly known as sewer gas, is a smelly, toxic gas that could prove useful as a supplement to anesthesia. In tests on mice, sewer gas caused suspended animation. This means the body's metabolism shuts down while the vital organs continue to work, but just barely. Even though the heart rate of the test mice decreased, the blood oxygen levels did not change. After ten minutes of induction, the mice showed these slowed effects. They returned to normal metabolic rates after 30 minutes of a normal air supply.[3] The benefit of suspended animation is in keeping organs functioning even without an adequate supply of oxygen. Larger animals have not yet been studied. Scientists hypothesize that IV doses may be needed in larger animals to be effective.

McSleepy the Robot

It was a meeting of the mechanical minds. In 2008, doctors at the McGill University Health Centre in Canada introduced the world's first anesthesia robot, nicknamed McSleepy. Two years later, this anesthesia robot teamed up with DaVinci, a type of surgical robot, to perform the first completely robotic surgery. The prostate removal surgery took place at Montreal General Hospital. Doctors praised the precision and safety of using the robots in surgical procedures. They found the anesthesia robot useful in precisely administering anesthetics. It could be tailored to each patient and surgical procedure. As Dr. T. M. Hemmerling of McGill explained, "Automated anesthesia delivery via McSleepy guarantees the same high quality of care every time it is used, independent from the subjective level of expertise. It can be configured exactly to the specific needs of different surgeries, such as robotic surgery."[4] The McSleepy can be programmed to be fully automated or semiautomated. It operates using touch screen controls, and anesthesiologists can program in numerous patient characteristics.

imaging, and delivering drugs, including anesthetics, to specific areas of the body.

In general anesthesia, nanotechnology could possibly allow for more automation in anesthesia monitoring. The heart rate and blood pressure of a patient under general anesthesia are already monitored. Some scientists believe nanodevices could allow the nervous system itself to be monitored. The nanodevices would link to the nerves to detect nerve impulses and monitor them using a computer.

In addition, some scientists believe that in the future, dentists may be able to administer local anesthetics using nanodentistry. The method mimics something out of a science fiction movie, where the nanorobots are inserted near the crown of the tooth and travel through the surface into the target site. This is just one example of nanorobots' future use—better and more specific drug targeting. Better

As robotics becomes increasingly common in operating rooms, anesthesia will become increasingly automated.

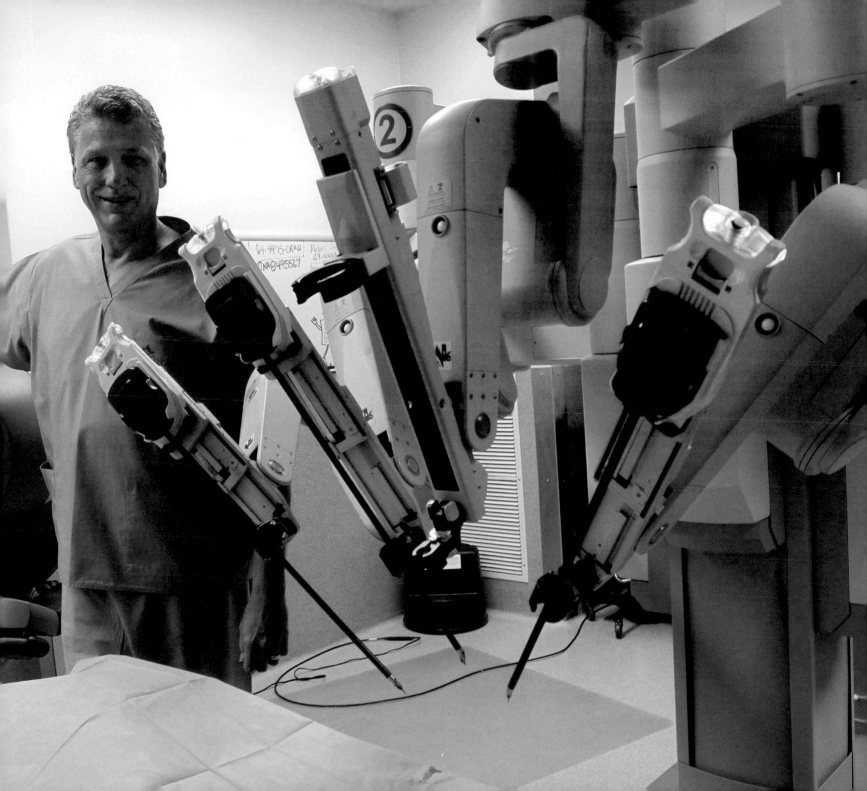

targeting equates to reduced doses, which means a lower chance of toxicity.

Anesthesia Outlook

Since William Morton administered ether anesthesia to Eben Frost in 1846, modern anesthesia has been constantly evolving. Since that amazing moment, childbirth analgesia and anesthesia, invasive surgeries, and even minor procedures have all become safer. The use of agents such as ether, chloroform, and halothane may have resulted in deaths or complications, but they only fueled further study to improve anesthesia care and safety. Scientists continue to study the pharmacological traits of the drugs, working to design precisely targeted, safer drugs. Studies in genetics and their effect on anesthesia will further customize the types of anesthetics patients receive. Researchers will continue to study the

"The fierce extremity of suffering has been steeped in the waters of forgetfulness and the deepest furrow in the knotted brow of agony has been smoothed for ever."[5]

—Oliver Wendell Holmes, American doctor and poet, speaking to the Harvard Medical College in 1847 on the invention of anesthesia

sensation of pain, working to find out more about the molecular mechanisms that drive it and how anesthetics affect them.

This research is ongoing, and with it, technology becomes an even more important aid to the well-trained anesthesiologist. Improving drugs, methods, and technology will continue with the patient in mind, and the future may hold just as many groundbreaking moments as the past 150 years.

✚ Timeline

3400 BCE

People in Mesopotamia grow the opium poppy for medicinal use.

ca. 1771

Joseph Priestley discovers nitrous oxide.

1805

Friedrich Sertürner discovers morphine, a chemical created from the seed pods of a poppy plant.

1821–1846

Massachusetts General Hospital performs fewer than one surgery per month.

1842

Dr. Crawford Long works with ether in October but does not publicize his results.

late 1800s

Adolf von Baeyer develops the first barbiturates.

1912

The American Medical Association Committee on Anesthesia rules chloroform is too risky for use.

1926

Mayo Clinic doctor John Lundy introduces balanced anesthesia, a technique that combines multiple types of anesthetic.

1932

Hexobarbital is first used for oral surgery in the United States.

1945

Niels Bjorn Jorgensen and Forrest Leffingwell develop the Jorgensen technique using multiple anesthesia agents.

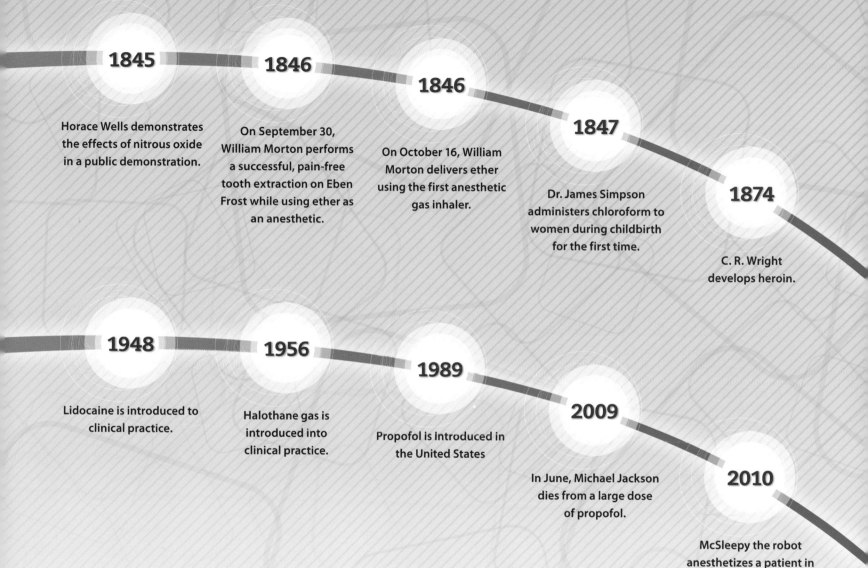

1845

Horace Wells demonstrates the effects of nitrous oxide in a public demonstration.

1846

On September 30, William Morton performs a successful, pain-free tooth extraction on Eben Frost while using ether as an anesthetic.

1846

On October 16, William Morton delivers ether using the first anesthetic gas inhaler.

1847

Dr. James Simpson administers chloroform to women during childbirth for the first time.

1874

C. R. Wright develops heroin.

1948

Lidocaine is introduced to clinical practice.

1956

Halothane gas is introduced into clinical practice.

1989

Propofol is Introduced in the United States

2009

In June, Michael Jackson dies from a large dose of propofol.

2010

McSleepy the robot anesthetizes a patient in the first all-robot surgery.

Glossary

amnesia

The loss of memory; a characteristic of general anesthesia.

analgesic

Any drug used to relieve pain.

barbiturate

An anesthetic drug that acts primarily as a central nervous system depressant, resulting in sedation in patients.

inflammation

A biological response from the body, often resulting in redness, heat, or swelling of a particular area of the body.

intravenous

Entering through or taking place in a vein.

metabolism

The process by which a living thing turns its food into energy.

neuropathy

A disease of the nerves.

obstetrician

A doctor who specializes in the management of women's health, particularly pregnancy, labor, and birth.

opioid

A drug derived from the opium poppy, also known as a narcotic, which binds to the opioid receptors in the central and peripheral nervous systems and gastrointestinal tract.

pharmacology

The study of drug action, including how drugs affect the body and how the body processes drugs.

placebo effect

The improvement in health or behavior not attributed to actual medicine but to the anticipation that a treatment will help.

potency

The strength of a particular drug in terms of the amount needed to achieve a desired effect.

respiratory

Having to do with breathing.

soluble

The ability to be dissolved in fatty tissues (lipids) or water.

stimulant

A drug that increases physical and mental functions, including alertness and wakefulness.

volatile

Rapidly evaporating.

✚ Additional Resources

Selected Bibliography

Smith, Tim, et al. *Fundamentals of Anaesthesia*. 3rd ed. New York: Cambridge UP, 2009. Print.

Snow, Stephanie J. *Blessed Days of Anaesthesia*. New York: Oxford UP, 2008. Print.

Stoelting, Robert K., and Ronald D. Miller. *Basics of Anesthesia*. 5th ed. Philadelphia: Churchill Livingstone, 2007. Print.

Further Readings

Dendy, Leslie, and Mel Boring. *Guinea Pig Scientists*. New York: Holt, 2005. Print.

Lace, William. *Anesthetics*. San Diego, CA: Lucent, 2004. Print.

Web Sites

To learn more about anesthetics, visit ABDO Publishing Company online at **www.abdopublishing.com**. Web sites about anesthetics are featured on our Book Links page. These links are routinely monitored and updated to provide the most current information available.

For More Information

The American Medical Association
515 N. State Street
Chicago, IL 60654
800-621-8335
http://www.ama-assn.org

The AMA's Web site provides a valuable resource for general medical information and is a good start for medical research.

The Mayo Clinic
200 First Street SW
Rochester, MN 55905
507-284-2511
http://www.mayo.edu/education/minnesota

The Mayo Clinic in Rochester has an extensive medical library available for use by visiting students.

The University of Minnesota Biomedical Library
505 Essex Street SE
Minneapolis, MN 55455
612-626-4045
http://hsl.lib.umn.edu/biomed

The biomedical library of the University of Minnesota, one of the top medical schools in the country, houses an enormous collection of resources.

✚ Source Notes

Chapter 1. Oral Surgery: Past and Present

1. C. D. T. James. "Mesmerism: A Prelude to Anaesthesia." *Proceedings of the Royal Society of Medicine* 68 (July 1975): 446. PMC, *US National Library of Medicine, National Institutes of Health*. Web. 20 Apr. 2013.

2. "Revealed: The 18th Century Guide to Amputations, Operations and Other Medical Tips." *Mail Online.* Daily Mail, 28 Jan. 2009. Web. 30 Apr. 2013.

3. "Getting Your Mouth Numbed at the Dentist." *Salt Lake City Dentist Blog.* Legacy Dental, 26 Dec. 2011. Web. 20 Apr. 2013.

4. John T. Sullivan. "Surgery Before Anesthesia." *Neurological Service, Massachusetts General Hospital.* MGH Neurological Service, n.d. Web. 30 Apr. 2013.

Chapter 2. How Anesthetics Work

1. Gifford Lum and Barry Mushlin. "Urine Drug Testing: Approaches to Screening and Confirmation Testing." *Laboratory Medicine* 6.35 (2004): 368. Print.

2. "IASP Taxonomy: Pain Terms." *International Association for the Study of Pain.* International Association for the Study of Pain, 22 May 2012. Web. 30 Apr. 2013.

3. Joshua Lang. "Awakening." *Atlantic.* Atlantic Monthly Group, 2 Jan. 2013. Web. 30 Apr. 2013.

Chapter 3. General Anesthesia: Going to Sleep

1. Stephanie J. Snow. *Blessed Days of Anaesthesia.* New York: Oxford UP, 2008. Print. 146.

2. Ibid. 172.

3. Ibid. 114.

4. Ibid. 115.

5. Morris S. Clark and Ann L. Brunick. *Handbook of Nitrous Oxide and Oxygen Sedation.* 3rd ed. Saint Louis, MO: Elsevier, 2008. Print. 6.

6. Ibid.

7. "Sevoflurane (Inhalation-Systemic)." *Drugs.com.* Drugs.com, n.d. Web. 20 Apr. 2013.

8. Daniel E. Becker and Morton Rosenberg. "Nitrous Oxide and the Inhalation Anesthetics." *Anesthesia Progress* 55.4 (Winter 2008): table 1. *PMC, US National Library of Medicine, National Institutes of Health.* Web. 20 Apr. 2013.

Chapter 4. Local Anesthetics: Alert, Without Sensation

1. Neal, Joseph M. "Effects of Epinephrine in Local Anesthetics on the Central and Peripheral Nervous Systems: Neurotoxicity and Neural Blood Flow." *Regional Anaesthesia and Pain Medicine* 28.3 (2003): 124. *American Society of Regional Anesthesia and Pain Medicine*. Web. 30 Apr. 2013.

2. "Local Anesthetics Used for Spinal Anesthesia." *International Federation of Nurse Anesthetists*. INFA, n.d. Web. 30 Apr. 2013.

3. Ibid.

4. John A. Yagiela. "Office-Based Anesthesia in Dentistry: Past, Present, and Future Trends." *Anesthesia in Dentistry* 43.2 (Apr. 1999): 208. Print.

5. Ibid.

6. Ibid. 207.

7. Ibid. 204.

8. Stephanie J. Snow. *Blessed Days of Anaesthesia*. New York: Oxford UP, 2008. Print. 78.

9. Ibid. 77.

10. "Combined Spinal-Epidural Anesthesia." *NYSORA*. New York School of Regional Anesthesia, 3 Aug. 2009. Web. 30 Apr. 2013.

Chapter 5. Pain-Free and Relaxed

1. Merlin Larson. "Richard C. Gill and the Introduction of Curare into Anesthesia Practice." *CSA Bulletin* 52.3 (July–September 2003): 48. *California Society of Anesthesiologists*. Web. 30 Apr. 2013.

Chapter 6. Anesthesia Techniques and Technology

None.

Chapter 7. Issues in Anesthesia

1. Caleb Ing. "Long-Term Differences in Language and Cognitive Function after Childhood Exposure to Anesthesia." *Pediatrics* 130.3 (2012): 476. Web. 30 Apr. 2013.

2. "Opiate Addiction in the United States." *National Institute on Drug Abuse*. National Institutes of Health, Aug. 2006. Web. 30 Apr. 2013.

3. Beverly A. Orser. "Lifting the Fog Around Anesthesia." *Scientific American* June 2007: 54. EBSCO Host. Web. 30 Apr. 2013.

4. "Informed Consent in the Operating Room." *Ethics in Medicine*. University of Washington School of Medicine, 1998. Web. 30 Apr. 2013.

Source Notes Continued

Chapter 8. Advancements and the Future

1. Beverly A. Orser. "Lifting the Fog Around Anesthesia." *Scientific American* June 2007: 60. *EBSCO Host*. Web. 30 Apr. 2013.

2. Gold, Jeffrey, et.al. "Virtual Anesthesia: The Use of Virtual Reality for Pain Distraction during Acute Medical Interventions." *Seminars in Anesthesia, Perioperative Medicine and Pain* 24.4 (Dec. 2005): 204. Web. 30 Apr. 2013.

3. "'Suspended Animation' Induced In Mice With Sewer Gas: Effects Are Reversible." *ScienceDaily*. ScienceDaily, 25 Mar. 2008. Web. 30 Apr. 2013.

4. McGill University Health Centre. "McSleepy Meets DaVinci: Doctors Conduct First-Ever All-Robotic Surgery and Anesthesia." *ScienceDaily*. ScienceDaily, 20 Oct. 2010. Web. 30 Apr. 2013.

5. William MacCormac. *The Hunterian Oration*. London, 1889. 52. *Google Book Search*. Web. 30 Apr. 2013.

✚ Index Continued

About the Author

Stephen Burgdorf works as an academic editor for a large university and does freelance writing and editing of books and magazines. He has done extensive interviewing and writing about individuals for his alumni magazine, *BUZZ Magazine,* and was the managing editor for the 2011–2013 editions of *Journeys: An Anthology of Adult Student Writing,* a book published yearly by the Minnesota Literacy Council.